A PASSION FOR THE FAMILY

A Passion for the Family

Bringing God's Love into the Home

Robert Ireton

Hodder & Stoughton

LONDON SYDNEY AUCKLAND TORONTO

Scripture taken from the HOLY BIBLE, NEW INTERNATIONAL
VERSION. Copyright © 1973, 1978, 1984 by International Bible
Society. Used by permission of International Bible Society and
Hodder and Stoughton, a division of Hodder Headline PLC.
All rights reserved.

First published in Great Britain 1996

10 9 8 7 6 5 4 3 2 1

British Library Cataloguing in Publication Data
A record for this book is available from the British Library

ISBN 0 340 64302 1

Printed and bound in Great Britain by
Cox & Wyman Ltd, Reading, Berks

Hodder and Stoughton Ltd
A Division of Hodder Headline PLC
338 Euston Road
London NW1 3BH

CONTENTS

Note: unless otherwise attributed, quotations are from the New International Version of the Bible. Abbreviations used for other versions are:

RSV = Revised Standard Version
TEV = Today's English Version (Good News Bible)
ICB = International Children's Bible (New Century Version)
JB = Jerusalem Bible

ACKNOWLEDGMENTS

My thanks go to the family of people who have supported me in the writing of this book. To the Rev. David Field who first put the idea in my head. To Carolyn and James at Hodders whose friendly and professional expertise has made that idea take shape. To the Rev. Mike Butterworth whose advice I have greatly valued. To Gill, Maria and Deryth whose typing skills saved the day. To my friends at Bishop Ridley Church and elsewhere who have prayed for me and recognised God's hand on this project. To Peter and Hilary Brand who have suffered with me for many hours at the hands of my computer and given such sound and practical advice. To my parents who taught me such a lot about family life. And above all to Barbara, Nathaniel, Samuel, Elliott and Elizabeth, without whom I could never have written this.

May what follows be to the glory of God and help others to be inspired by a passion for the family.

PREFACE

I was born an idealist. All my life I have sought after perfection. Even at the age of five my shiny soap-scrubbed face and red bow-tie were a give-away. I looked at the world with great expectations. As I grew up this started to change. Little by little my idealism was challenged by the realities of life: the threat of nuclear wipe-out in the Cuban missile crisis; the human tragedies of Biafra and Aberfan; the political scandals of Profumo and Watergate; and the economic scandals of unemployment, poverty, oil crisis, inflation. All these things had a deep effect on me and made me more determined than ever to search for something better.

Today I am still an idealist. But the focus of my idealism has changed. I no longer believe that economics, politics, or the world in general has the answer to human needs. Since Christ came into my life my idealism has stopped being a question of: 'What can I do about the way things are?', and has become a question of: 'What can God do about them?' This has changed my whole perspective on the world. I now realise that God isn't interested in patching up the mess that human beings have made of his world; he's in the business of remaking it and them all over again. He got started on this plan the moment the first family was exiled from his paradise; he followed it through human history until the moment came for him to enter the human family in person; and when he entered that family he showed to everyone who met him that with God all things were possible.

Bringing Christ into the family doesn't provide an instant solution to every human need: it restores to our homes the passion for a paradise which some of us thought was lost for good.

1

HELP!

It's five minutes past eight on a Thursday morning. Elliott, aged eleven, has just put his foot in a sandwich and has now sat in the butter. My wife, Barbara, who teaches at a local infant school, should be leaving for work in a few minutes and we haven't even started breakfast.

As I come to the table, the tell-tale remains of crunched cornflakes all over the floor remind me that my eldest son Nathaniel (fourteen) has been here before me. Meanwhile Elizabeth (nine) and Samuel (twelve) are having a passionate debate about who is most worthy to receive the last portion of Cornpops!

We are rapidly running out of time. Half the breakfast things are missing from the table; the milk, left out from Nathaniel's breakfast forty minutes earlier, is lukewarm; and my patience with three irritable young people has snapped. '*Will you be quiet!*' I bellow.

An eerie silence falls on the room. The children sit. Dad says a heavy-hearted 'Thank you for our food' prayer and a hasty breakfast-time begins. 'What a way to start the day,' I say to myself. Aloud I say, 'If this happens tomorrow there's going to be trouble. You know the drill. You should all be sitting at the table with your cereals out by eight o'clock at the latest.'

Breakfast is one of my favourite meals, but not like this. I need help; I can't believe that this is how family life is meant to be. It was never like this in *The Cosby Show* or in *The Waltons*. These family soap operas make parenthood seem so much easier.

I wonder what your family life is like. Have you ever thought,

'Help! I can't stand any more of this'? You get up earlier; you pray more; you organise and plan ahead more; you nag the children; you moan at your partner; you try the 'Here endeth the last and final lesson' approach at the meal table. However, all your attempts to produce the sort of family life you would really like to have seem to be failing.

To make matters worse, you notice that other people seem to be making a better job of parenthood than you. Succeeding at this game of family life looks about as likely as winning the jackpot on the National Lottery.

Writing a book on the family is a risky business. There is a danger that you will think I'm an expert, someone who has 'made it' as far as family life is concerned. Let me assure you I haven't. This book is the result of my search for some answers to the issues that all of us who live in families face.

It is a search that has gone on for a long time, in many different places and continues to challenge me more than any-thing else I do in life. And it has led to an exciting discovery: *bringing Christ into our home can really make a difference to our family life*.

Asking for help

I am not very good at DIY. I try hard, but sometimes everything seems to go wrong. On one occasion I did try to get some help, but not until my pride was exhausted. The job seemed simple enough.

The chain on Elliott's mountain bike had broken. One of the links had come adrift and needed clipping back together. 'I can do this,' I said to myself, even though I had never made a repair like this before.

Half an hour later I had worked up such a head of steam that I felt like flinging the bike across the garden. I just couldn't get the repair to work. Eventually Barbara heard the gathering storm in the garden and came out to lend a hand.

'Why didn't you come out to help before?' I snapped.

'Why didn't you ask for my help if you needed it!?' she replied.

That was a good question. I realised five minutes into the repair job that I needed another pair of adult hands. But I had failed to ask for help.

Before we can begin to experience the difference Christ can make in our homes, we need to ask for his help. This sounds so obvious, but I have found it to be one of the biggest obstacles in my life. I am so independent! Many of us are. We're not good at asking for help.

When you think about it, most of our learning and maturing in life does not happen by chance; it actually comes through asking for things. The baby's nagging cry asks for comfort; the toddler's outstretched hand asks for food; the three-year-old's climb into Dad's lap, armed with a book, asks for a story; the five-year-old's endless questions about the very nature of the universe itself ask for some straight answers. Asking for help is a way of life for children. They literally thrive on it. When we grow up all this starts to change. Adulthood means we're ready to make it on our own, depend on our own resources, our own energies and our own lives. By the time we've reached the age of eighteen self-reliance has become highly prized. This is a pity.

I don't think that's how Jesus saw things at all. He once had a historic interview with a very self-reliant man. St John tells us about it in chapter 3 of his gospel.

Springtime had returned to the hills around Jerusalem. Pilgrims were flooding into the city for Passover, stopping occasionally to admire the blossom-laden groves of fruit trees. It was a beautiful and exciting place to be at that time of year; no wonder so many people travelled from all over Israel to be there for the feast.

Jesus was among them, travelling with his loyal group of friends. His teaching and amazing power to help people added to the excitement of this particular Passover. His name was the buzz word on every street corner. So it was that one evening a man called Nicodemus made his way along alleys and back streets to meet Jesus privately.

The cover of darkness made Nicodemus feel secure. He was a Pharisee – one of the religious elite; it wouldn't do for him to be seen openly talking to someone who was regarded by his colleagues as a maverick. If word got out, he might lose his seat on the ruling council. His religious career would be finished. But seeking help from Jesus meant taking this risk, and Nicodemus felt his journey was worth it.

Jesus fascinated him. Here was a man who had spiritual clout. He not only taught people the ways of God, he also showed them what God could do. The city was alive with the rumours of 'water into wine' at a wedding feast in the north. The story sounded a bit far-fetched and yet people here in Jerusalem had seen him cure people without medicine before their very eyes. There was something special about this man, and Nicodemus wanted to find out more.

Jesus was ready for the appointment when Nicodemus arrived. He didn't hate Pharisees, but he knew they were good at waffling and getting off the point when he was getting the better of them. So, as this highly educated man began his set piece, Jesus interrupted him and came straight to the point: '. . . I tell you the truth, unless a man is born again, he cannot see the kingdom of God' (John 3:3).

No beating about the bush in this statement; no getting into long complicated discussions about points of law. Born again. Nicodemus had to be born all over again. He wondered what this meant.

Nicodemus felt safe with rules and procedures. Like the rest of his religious party, he knew the rules and spent his whole life trying to keep them. But being born again? This was ridiculous. He couldn't see how a man of his age and experience could make a new start and begin his spiritual journey all over again – as if he were a baby. Turning water into wine and healing people was one thing, but spiritual life was another.

'How can a man be born when he is old?' Nicodemus asked (John 3:4). He believed he was too old to change.

'Too old to change'. I've heard that expression a few times. It doesn't always come in those exact words. A mother said to me, 'It's too late,' when she saw her teenage son completely out of control. A dad said to me, 'It's impossible; I can't turn the clock back,' when he realised that he had missed many precious moments in the lives of his new grown-up children.

Like Nicodemus we look at ourselves, our resources and our way of doing things, and conclude that nothing can be done. We're trapped in the consequences of what we have done in the past, and cannot see a way to start all over again. Humanly speaking this may well be true. Listen to Sandy's story.

Sandy came to me one day in quite a state. Her eight-year-old son Sean was in serious trouble. I knew the family well. They lived on a farm on the edge of a country town. Sandy and her husband Bill worked long hours in their struggle to make ends meet in an economic recession. They weren't committed Christians but they were both good people, and I knew them to be good parents to their three children.

I listened as Sandy poured out her story. Sean was a terror. He was hyperactive and had periods of uncontrollable behaviour. She had first come to see me about this when he was three years old. We had talked and prayed about the problem, and Jesus had answered our prayers very directly; there had been a definite improvement in Sean's behaviour.

Her eyes filled up as she showed a photograph of him five years on. His bright blue eyes sparkled under a head of dark brown hair. He looked so smart in his school uniform. It was hard to believe that this was the same boy who had recently almost demolished one of his father's barns with a fork-lift truck!

Humanly speaking it looked as if nothing could be done for Sean. Sandy and Bill had tried medical help and received family counselling. They'd even tried putting him on a special diet, which he loathed. Nothing worked. At three years old he was small enough to pick up and restrain; this had become impractical five years on.

As I handed Sandy a box of tissues, I felt powerless to help any of them. But as I prayed with her, we spoke to someone who wasn't. Bringing Christ into Sandy and Bill's family situation had made a difference before, and I believed he could once again change things.

Asking Christ for help does not guarantee things will work out as we want them to, but it does mean we gain access to resources beyond ourselves: 'And my God will meet all your needs according to his glorious riches in Christ Jesus' (Phil. 4:19).

Sometimes God has to let us get to the point of crisis before we are ready to let him into a situation we cannot change. I don't know exactly how Jesus is going to answer our prayers for Sean this time round, but I know we can trust him. All may seem lost and hopeless, but with Christ in the situation it isn't.

Facing the facts

I remember a particularly horrible Friday evening. It didn't start out badly; in fact, it was one of those rare days when all the children got on well together. They played in their rooms without declaring World War III on each other and tidied up when it was time to get ready for a weekend away. They didn't even argue about who was going to sit in the back of our seven-seater, three-row car.

As we drove off down the motorway, I allowed myself the luxury of a few moments of parental pride: perhaps after all, our struggles to teach them to co-operate with and love one another were finally beginning to pay off. We stopped for tea at one of our favourite road-side restaurants: burgers and chips never tasted so good. It felt great to be a family. But something happened when we reached our destination. It started the moment the children got out of the car. Call it tiredness, or silly behaviour, or high spirits ... call it what you like. Their horrible behaviour spoiled what would otherwise have been a perfect day.

'How could you!' I exploded when they were ready for bed. 'How could you spoil such a wonderful day?' I sat there staring at them in the icy silence. They said nothing, but in any case I was in no mood to listen to anything they might have to say. I just couldn't face them.

I left the room feeling a failure and imagined myself writing out my resignation from this job of being a parent. 'Why does it have to hurt so much?' I asked myself and God.

The fact is, being a parent and running a family isn't easy. It is full of ups and downs. There are no easy, instant solutions. But I have found that things go a lot better when I am honest with God and my family about how I am feeling about what is going on.

That Friday night I felt unwilling to forgive and forget. My hopes and expectations had been shattered; I needed space to think things through. I put our relationship as a family on 'hold' until I had grace from God to try again.

There is nothing wrong with admitting your need to do this from time to time: to face the fact of your failure and mistakes and give yourselve and your family some breathing space. Failure only becomes a serious problem when we can't or won't accept that we are not yet perfect, and neither are our loved ones. The apostle Paul, urging Christians to put their confidence in Christ rather than themselves, put it like this:

> And we all ... are being changed into his likeness from one degree of glory to another; for this comes from the Lord who is the Spirit (2 Cor. 3:18 RSV).

Sometimes these degrees of change come about painfully slowly. In the plan and purposes of God, the speed of change is not important. Like Nicodemus, we simply need to turn the whole of our lives over to him, including our home life.

Finding the key

My home is in a particularly vulnerable place. I live in a vicarage three feet away from the east-end wall of the church on one side and right next to a children's playground on the other. This makes it exposed for two reasons.

First, its closeness to the church is a constant reminder that our home life is on show. Members of the church and the local community can see how we live and make judgments about our family life. There is nothing wrong with this in principle. But in practice the conclusions sometimes drawn are completely wrong.

For instance, Elizabeth came home from school one day and told us her friends thought we must be very rich.

'Why is that, Elizabeth?' I asked.

'Well, they think we must be very rich because we live in such a big house,' she replied.

This made me laugh. Although our house happens to be the largest in the parish, it doesn't belong to me. Given our income at the time, we couldn't have afforded to buy a garage in the area, let alone a house!

Sometimes the comments that are made about the way we live are rather more difficult to laugh off. When people say, 'You're not going on holiday *again* are you?', I try to smile sweetly and avoid the 'I am perfectly justified in having a break, and anyway it's none of your business' routine. But comments like this hurt all the same.

Some clergy craftily plan their holidays to start on a Monday and finish the following Saturday so that as few people in the church as possible will know they're away. I've tried to be as open as possible with people about the fact that holidays for us have to be away from the vicarage.

Clergy don't live 'over the shop', they live in the shop. My work constantly intrudes on and interrupts my home life. I love my work, but if I want to get a break from it and have time alone with my family, the vicarage is not the place to do it. 'Don't let the church cast too dark a shadow over the vicarage,' Bishop David Say told me before I began parish ministry. This has proved to be very sound advice indeed.

Your house may be quite different from mine; you may not live in your place of work and you may be free to choose, within reason, where you live. However, we all have to live with other people's expectations of us. Auntie perhaps expects our children to behave in church like hers did twenty years ago. Mother-in-law might expect us to visit on her terms and in her home if we want our children to see their grandparents: then she wonders why they spill blackcurrant on her nice white carpet, drop food over the posh upholstered dining suite and treat her sacred porcelain like jumble sale toys. People's expectations of us can make us feel we're in a prison. Let me illustrate what I mean.

Sunday afternoons at theological college were like a bad dream for me. I came to dread them. In those days students were placed in churches all over North London. Along with our families we attended a different church every Sunday during the year of our placement. This meant a lot of travelling for some people. Unsuspecting victims in the congregation (my description, not theirs) were asked to volunteer to host us for Sunday lunch.

The idea was good in theory. It meant you could talk to members of the congregation and get to know them a bit better. In practice it was a nightmare. The sensible ones at college voted with their feet and stayed at home!

We had three children under five at the time. Imagine taking pram, high chair, Milupa and everything else besides to a different home each Sunday and trying to have a spiritual conversation with anyone. Poor Barbara, I don't know how she stuck it.

The expectations all this placed upon families were totally unreasonable. Family life needs supporting and this kind of over-exposure is unlikely to do much to strengthen or help it.

Our homes are all unique places because each of us is different. God planned it that way. I'm sure some people at college thought Sunday arrangements were great: no lunch to cook, a different home to go to each week, other children for theirs to play with and the chance to have a spiritual 'heart-to-heart' with someone they felt drawn to counsel. For others of us it was not quite that simple.

If you're anything like me, you have enough trouble trying to live up to your own expectations without having to follow the customs of others. They may know nothing of the personal struggles you're facing.

The key to asking for and finding help in our homes is held by Christ. It is not a question of what other people expect of us but what *he* requires of us. I suspect many of us have expectations of our families which are wholly unrealistic. We know what we want our family life to be like, and dream of how it might become like this. Christ needs to interrupt this sort of fantasy and bring us face to face with the way he sees things. Then we can be freed from the prison of other people's expectations. And Christ can help us become what he made us to be.

Keeping evil out

The other reason our home is a vulnerable place is because it borders on a concrete playground. This looked promising when we first moved in. The vicarage garden (untypically) is tiny and quite unsuitable for growing children's idea of 'play'. Having a playground on our doorstep seemed a great idea. But the missiles changed all that.

The first one came over the fence in early spring in 1991. As I cut the lawn one afternoon, a tin can came hurtling over the six-foot wooden fence. I ignored it and continued to push the noisy electric machine around the lawn. Next came more litter – a bottle, leftover food, sticks and some bits of broken plastic in various shapes and sizes. Finally a large public litter bin flew through the air and landed a few feet away. Someone was trying to give me a message. By this stage they certainly had my attention. As I made my way to the park thinking of what might have happened if the bin had hit one of the children, steam was coming out of my ears and fire from my mouth.

Since those early days, missiles continue to arrive from out of the sky. We've only had one attempt to set fire to the house – so far – and honestly the neighbourhood isn't as bad as some of this sounds. These incidents have taught me an important lesson: *our homes are targets for the evil one to throw all sorts of rubbish at.* They are not neutral territory and none of us live as Christians in peace-time. We need to recognise that some of our struggles are not what they appear to be.

Coming to this conclusion has taken me far too long in terms of family life, and I find that I need to be constantly reminded about it.

For we are not fighting against human beings but against the
wicked spiritual forces in the heavenly world, the rulers, authorities, and cosmic powers of this dark age (Eph. 6:12 TEV).

It is no coincidence that St Paul wrote these words in the
context of his teaching about the family. They have much to
teach us about the unseen pressures which are at work to
undermine our families.

This truth was brought home forcibly to me in a conversation
I recently had with a seven-year-old boy. I met him in a
department store in the high street. His mother was busy
shopping and he had gone off to the toy counter.

I know Daniel well. He lives around the corner from me and
goes to the local school. It was Easter holidays, and I asked him
whether he was enjoying his break from school. Then without
warning he asked me, 'Is Weegy true, Robert?'

It was the last question I expected from this innocent-looking
child. What was he doing asking me a question like that at his
age? Recovering from the shock, I tried to explain to him about
the dangers of this evil game as simply as I could. It turned out
that some of his friends had encouraged him to play with a ouija
board with them.

Daniel's parents had warned him to have nothing to do with
what they called the 'Black Arts'. However, he had asked me this
question just to make sure that his mum and dad were telling
him the truth.

Some of the things that happen to us are just part of the
ordinary struggles that any family can expect to go through.
However, as Christians we need to tune in to the spiritual battle
that all of us are called to fight. This means recognising that evil
is at work in our world and taking action to stop it getting a grip
on us or our children.

At every infant baptism service that I take in my role as an
Anglican clergyman, I say to parents and godparents: 'It is your
duty to bring up this child/these children to fight against evil and
to follow Christ.'[1] Some of us are better at remembering the
'following Christ' bit than the 'fighting against evil'. Our homes

are targets for the evil one. We need to seek Christ's help to keep evil out.

Letting Christ in

Until recently all of our children have had to rely on Barbara or me to let them into the house. There are good reasons for this. Safety in the home is very important. It means that an adult is always around when they are in the house. This is particularly important when it comes to answering the door. We occasionally get some strange people turning up on our vicarage doorstep or in our garden.

On one occasion I went to investigate strange noises in the front garden. It was after dark but I could make out the shape of two people lying in the bushes, just a few metres from our lounge window. They were trying to have sex; I say 'trying' because they were both very drunk and were (fortunately) having some difficulty taking off each other's clothes.

The couple weren't bothered by my presence, and would have carried on having sex right in front of me if I hadn't insisted they leave. Even when they finally staggered out the garden gate, the sounds on the other side of the fence told me they had no intention of stopping what they had started. I have good reason to be wary about our children's safety.

We have delayed giving our children a key to the house for as long as possible. This has caused problems for our eldest son Nathaniel because, until recently, he has usually been home before anyone else gets in. When this has happened he has had to wait or go to a neighbour for an emergency key. But on his fourteenth birthday we presented Nathaniel with a front-door key. He had a lot more exciting presents than this slim shining piece of metal, but as I gave it to him I said:

What I am about to give you Nathaniel is one of the most important and valuable presents Mum and I can ever entrust you with. This piece of metal gives you access to our home. It means you can get in and out without us being there. It means we trust you to look after the house when we're not around. It is given to you on trust. Don't ever use it to let someone or something into our home that Christ wouldn't want there.

This was a rather grand and exaggerated statement, looking back on it. In practice Barbara and I are still very cautious of leaving Nathaniel in the house on his own for any length of time. We trust him, but only so far. He does not yet have the maturity or experience to be left completely to his own devices.

However, this incident helps to show us something important. For the Christian faith to make any difference in our homes we have to let Christ in. We need to, as it were, hand him the key to our home and give him the right of access. When we do this two amazing things happen.

1   Jesus moves in to live with us as we are, not as we would like to be. We love having people to stay or come to visit for the day. There is something very rewarding about sharing your home, particularly when it is shared with someone who has no children or family of their own. Before a visitor comes we try to make sure that our home is welcoming. The children all pitch in and help to tidy up. We don't spring clean, but we do like the place to be presentable.

Sometimes we have unexpected guests. When they phone to say they're coming, I always tell them, 'Fine, but you'll have to take us as you find us.' That's precisely what happens when we let Christ in. When Christ moves into our homes and families he does not require us to clean or tidy up first. He takes our family as he finds it. All he requires of us is that we make him feel welcome.

2   Jesus does not change the locks! He has the right to. St John reminds us: 'Through him all things were made; without him nothing was made that has been made' (John 1:3). Our homes and families owe their existence to God's creation through Christ. All things rightfully belong to Christ and by letting him into our homes we are merely allowing him access to what is already his.

Yet the amazing thing is that when Christ comes in it is not a takeover but a partnership. Letting Christ in is only the beginning. It's like the born-again experience Jesus taught Nicodemus about. It's the beginning of a process which is not under our control but does not take over control of us. We still retain the right to bolt the door and deny Christ access or to prevent him getting into rooms and areas of our lives we'd rather he didn't see. That's fine. Christ is a patient Lord, and he doesn't barge his way into any areas of our homes or families where he is not made welcome. But he does long to come in. He longs to make our homes his home, our struggles his struggles, our blessings and joys his remedy for other families that are going down under the waters of despair for the last time. Jesus Christ makes everything possible. He is such an amazing and wonderful homemaker. Let's look now at some of the things he can do with us in ours.

2

HOME TRUTHS

I have lived in twenty-three different homes in thirty-eight years. That's an average of 1.6 years in each place. All my homes have been very different. One was a flat, another a council house. I've sampled what it's like to live in a beautiful five-storey eighteenth-century mansion and to sleep in a coverted garden shed. For me home is where I am living at the moment. This may not always be an ideal place.

The worst experience Barbara and I have had of making a house into a home was when we moved into temporary accommodation. The house itself was lovely, a four-bedroomed dormer bungalow with stunning views of the Lakeland Fells. But it was very difficult to call 'Trevellyan' our home. It was only going to be ours for a few months (or so we thought). The vicarage we were supposed to be moving into had to undergo major repairs before we could live in it. I wrote to the Bishop to complain. He was very understanding but explained why this had to be done. I told God I didn't want to move three hundred and twenty miles north from London only to move all over again a few months later. He was very understanding too. But it didn't change the fact that a home in the vicarage at Matterdale would have to wait. I shall always remember the day it came to laying the carpets. I held the hammer in one hand and the tacks in the other. I just couldn't bring myself to nail them in. 'What's the point?' I said to Barbara. 'We'll have to take them up again soon.'

In the end, after days of indecision I went to work with the hammer. Just as well. We were there for much longer than the three to six months we had been told it would take to get the vicarage finished.

Our experience of making a home in 'Trevellyan' taught me an important truth. In reality we all live in temporary accommodation. 'For here we have no permanent home' as the writer of Hebrews puts it (Heb. 13:14).

For some of us 'temporary' will mean a few days, weeks or months. For others it may mean sixty years, or more. We have several friends in retirement who have lived in the same home all their lives. Others, like me, are still counting! But wherever we live, however long we live there, Christ wants to be the perma- nent foundation of our home life. When we have a relationship with him in our families, we are beginning something that he wants to last for ever. This means making sure we're using materials that are going to last longer than a lifetime. Jesus spoke about this on the night before he died.

Twelve of Jesus's closest friends celebrated Passover with him that evening. It was to be a night they would never forget, although none of them realised it at the time. They were enjoying this special meal together. Jesus was so often surrounded by crowds wanting his attention. In this room they had him all to themselves.

Peter sensed the mood of the evening change when Jesus got up to do the slave's bit on their dirty feet. But neither he nor any of the others guessed what it all meant. Jesus knew this.

'You do not understand now what I am doing, but one day you will,' he said (John 13:7). Jesus sensed that they hadn't got it; the penny hadn't dropped. But he went on to share with them some of the most important words of his life.

He spoke a lot about homes. He made heaven sound like a place with your own luxury villa – or at least a five-star hotel big enough to accommodate the entire population of God's people throughout human history. It confused them a little. They couldn't understand how his father fitted into the picture, where he was about to go or why he wanted to limit himself to just them. Judas (not Iscariot) asked Jesus a question about this and his reply contained an important home truth: 'If anyone loves me, he will obey my teaching. My Father will love him, and we will come to him and make our home with him' (John 14:23).

Jesus wanted a relationship with his friends that was as close to home as possible. But this would not be achieved without some cost.

Camelot

I've begun to understand the real cost of a home a bit better since taking out a mortgage to buy 'Camelot', the first house we have ever owned. It's a lot easier to talk about making a home than to pay for it. The idea of having our own home was lovely. Here at last was somewhere to escape to as a family on our days off. Here was a home of our own where we could do as we pleased, a place to holiday in and build together while the children were still young enough to want to be with us, a special place to share with family and friends.

It had taken fifteen years to get to the point where buying a house became a possibility. On paper and in the estate agents' window it looked wonderful. But when Barbara and I sat down to work out how much 'Camelot' was going to cost us, we nearly gave up on the idea. Quite apart from the mortgage, there was the cost of getting a survey, employing a solicitor, furnishing the property, making the electrical system safe and repairing the central heating boiler. And on it went. It seemed at times like an endless drain on our bank account. It made an enormous dent in our savings. 'Camelot' was a very attractive home, but moving in cost us all we had.

Similarly, there is a great cost in following Jesus. But, like Jesus's first friends, many of us are attracted to him by his wonderful love. This was certainly true for me. I first became aware of his love at the age of ten, when I used to sing in a village church choir.

One year I was sent on a course run by the Royal School of Church Music in Taunton. I don't remember anything about the teaching, but I remember vividly the first night I was there.

We were all assembled in the chapel for a communion service

and I was beginning to feel very homesick. This was my first experience of being away from home on my own, and I wasn't enjoying it at all. The very 'high church' service included clouds and clouds of incense, making me feel even more sick! The incense wafted around the huge Victorian building and made my eyes water – they didn't need much encouragement to do that.

Soon loneliness welled up inside me like a wave about to break inside my chest.

Desperately trying to fight back the tears, I suddenly became aware that I wasn't alone. Of course there were hundreds of other people all around me, but I don't mean alone in that sense. I suddenly became aware of God putting his arms around me and giving me a large warm hug. I could not see him, but I knew he was there.

What followed was a sense of peace and stillness that I had never felt before. I had no idea what had happened to me and didn't understand it at the time. But I knew at that moment there was a God who loved me. I never needed to feel alone again. For the first time I began to understand what it meant to make my home in God's love (John 15:9).

We need to encounter and experience this love in our lives if our faith is to make any difference to what goes on in our homes. A set of beliefs, rules and regulations just isn't enough. There needs to be that personal meeting with the living God who made us and wants to breathe his love into us.

For each of us the way this happens will be different. It may happen dramatically like St Paul's experience on the road to Damascus (Acts 9:1–5). It may happen gradually over a long period of time like it has for me. But however it takes place, we need to meet with Jesus in a real and tangible way.

In the same room where Jesus told his disciples about wanting to make his home in them, he told them that he was the way to this sort of fullness of life (John 14:6). Through an encounter with Jesus we experience the height, breadth, length and depths of God's love. It is a love beyond our understanding. It is the real meaning of life. We can read about it, try to manufacture it, even borrow it from other people for a short time. But God's amazing love needs to enter into the most intimate place of our lives. When his love gets home to us in this way then we shall find the strength to go on when things get really tough and we are tempted to turn away from him.

Christ wants a permanent relationship with us that won't just see us through this life, but will take us through into eternity. This is not an easy, slushy sort of love we're talking about. It's a love that cost Christ everything, and if we are to share it then it will cost us too.

Solid foundations

When I was fourteen we moved house. This meant leaving the village and the choir I had belonged to since I was eight years old. It was a difficult moment for me. I was about to begin course-work at school for my O-levels and didn't want to face a change of schools and all that went with it. But, when I left the choir I was given something that could help me in my relationships with God and other people for the rest of my life. It was a Bible.

I tried to feel grateful for this present but instead I thought, 'How boring.' I put it on my bookshelf to prop up other books, and there it would have stayed if God hadn't taken a hand in things.

Five years later I was at teacher training college in Cheltenham. I took the Bible with me when I went, as a souvenir of my childhood. Sound familiar? I wonder if your Bible (if you have one) is just a souvenir from the past, propping up books or kept in place by sentimental feelings.

Then one day Marcus strolled into my room. He was tall, skinny and much more religious than I cared to be. But his honest friendship and Lancashire straight-talk got through to me. 'D'you ever read this book, Rob?' he asked, picking up my Bible from its place and catching the other books as they slid along the shelf. I tried to think of a clever answer, but for once I couldn't. 'No,' I said. 'It was given to me when I left the church choir.'

'Oh,' Marcus replied. Obviously he wasn't impressed. So I

added, 'Anyway, most of it isn't true. It was written thousands of
years ago and we can't possibly know whether anything in it can
be believed.' There was a long, awkward pause. My self-justifi-
cation had only made things worse.

'I believe Jesus was a real person, of course. But that's about
all. You don't have to believe in the Bible to believe in God,' I
added, desperately trying to dig myself out of a hole. Marcus was
very gracious. He didn't take me up on anything I had said at all.
He simply replied, 'Why don't you try reading it sometime.
There are a lot of good things in it.'

I never did find out what Marcus had come to see me about in
the first place. But that conversation had a lasting impact upon
me.

'God moves in a mysterious way, his wonders to perform.'[1]
From that moment I started to read the large green New English
Bible which I had been given four years earlier. The pages were
still sticky from lack of use, but God started to change that. I
didn't know what to make of most of what I read, and twenty
years on there is still a lot that I don't fully understand. But
thank God for friends like Marcus whom God sends into our
homes from time to time to get us back on track.

Let's get back to the upper room for a moment. Jesus wanted
his friends to follow him. They'd been through a lot together.
He'd taken care of them for three years. They'd experienced the
power of God's love in their lives. They'd seen this love at work
in the world.

Jesus wanted this to continue when he had left the room for
good. However, he wanted them to understand that following
him, being his disciple and friend and welcoming him into their
lives meant loving and obeying his Word. He knew this wouldn't
always be easy. And it isn't. 'You are my friends if you do what I
command you,' Jesus said (John 15:14): that means taking to
heart what we read in this holy book.

Learning to trust the truth

The Bible is a most fascinating book. It's unique. It was written over a period of sixteen hundred years during sixty generations. Its authors included a highly educated prince (Moses), a cowboy (Amos), a civil servant (Nehemiah), a labourer (Peter) and the equivalent of an Oxford don (Paul). Put that lot together and it's no wonder we find it hard to follow sometimes.

The Bible is a record book. It has been translated into more languages and read by more people than any other book in history: it's earned its place in the *Guinness Book of World Records*.

It's a very human book, full of all sorts of human emotions. There's the elation of Psalm 103: 'Praise the LORD, O my soul; all my inmost being, praise his holy name. Praise the LORD, O my soul, and forget not all his benefits.' Then there's the heartbreak of David in Psalm 51: 'Have mercy on me, O God, according to your unfailing love ... Against you, you only, have I sinned and done what is evil in your sight.' There's the cry of victory in the song of Moses: 'Who among the gods is like you, O LORD? Who is like you – majestic in holiness, awesome in glory, working wonders?' (Exod. 15:11) and then the blackness of despair in the depression of Job: 'O God, put a curse on the day I was born; put a curse on the night when I was conceived! Turn that day into darkness, God. Never again remember that day ...' (Job 3:3–4).

The Bible is full of real people and real families facing real problems. It's a true and trustworthy book. We shall find it a lot easier to obey if we have confidence that what it says is trustworthy. As we recognise its relevance to our lives today we shall come to value the advice it gives about the sorts of family issues we have to face.

Take the home life of Isaac and Rebecca, for instance. What a realistic case study their family makes. After a long time of trying to get pregnant, Rebecca eventually gave birth to twins: two boys named Esau and Jacob. From the start the two parents took sides in their homes. Isaac gave the eldest son Esau special treament at the expense of Jacob. Rebecca did the same for Jacob at the expense of Esau. The result was disastrous. The two brothers became dreadful rivals vying for their parents' affections. Things got so bad that on one occasion Jacob swindled Esau out of the family fortune.

Esau was a he-man, a macho figure. He was rough, tough and keen on outdoor pursuits. Jacob on the other hand was the exact opposite. He was a real smoothie, a 'mummy's boy'. He preferred to stay at home and help with the cooking. Esau probably thought he was a wimp. Being a man's man and one of the main breadwinners, Esau could do no wrong in his father's eyes.

When the day came for the family fortune to be divided up Esau had it made. Being the elder, he was guaranteed the lion's share of the estate. Jacob resented this and plotted against his brother. Ironically his chance came quite unexpectedly. You could say that it was handed to him on a plate.

One day while Jacob was in the kitchen cooking, Esau burst into the room. He was desperate for something to stuff his mouth with, and in his hurry to satisfy his appetite he ran straight into the jaws of his brother's trap. 'I'll swap you some food for your fortune,' was effectively what Jacob said to him.

Esau's brawn got the better of his brain. What did he care about his fortune? If he didn't get some food down himself soon he would never live to see it! 'Just give me some food. I'll agree to anything – just feed me,' he said to his cunning brother. With each gulp of the delicious home cooking, Esau swallowed Jacob's bait – hook, line and sinker.

What a story. Read it for yourself in Genesis 25. It has such a ring of truth about it, giving a powerful warning to parents who take sides. The Bible is full of true stories like this one. As we look at different issues families face we find that its message is so clear and relevant today.

St Paul said, 'All Scripture is God-breathed and is useful for teaching, rebuking, correcting and training in righteousness, so that the man of God may be thoroughly equipped for every good work' (2 Tim. 3:16). That includes everything from Genesis to

Revelation. As we plough the Bible's pages we shall reap a rich harvest of truth. We can trust its teaching on the family because it is reliable, trustworthy and true.

Starting from scratch

When I first took the Bible seriously I opened it at Genesis 1, verse 1 and started to read. I wouldn't recommend this as a good way of discovering home truths. It's more helpful to use a reading scheme such as the excellent ones produced by Scripture Union, Crusade for World Revival or Bible Reading Fellowship.

Whatever method you choose to help you to read what God says, don't skip over the opening chapters of Genesis. I have found more teaching on marriage and the family in these opening verses than almost anywhere else in the Bible; it repays careful study many times over.

In the opening book of the Bible we are given the opportunity to glimpse what an ideal home might look like. The first parents began life with a great advantage over the rest of us: they were perfect. Hard to imagine, isn't it?

Let's take a look at Dad first: he was God's first masterpiece. Genesis 2:7 tells us that God used very basic ingredients to make the first man. You and I call these ingredients atoms; the Bible calls them dust. However, we mustn't be fooled by the unprom-ising nature of such basic ingredients. The creation story of Genesis 1 makes it clear that human beings are special. God wasn't ready to make them until everything else was perfect.

In the beginning life was easy. All the father had to do in those days was the gardening. Everything else could be left to God. Imagine it: gardening with perfect growing conditions and no weeds or bugs. No wonder John Milton referred to this story as 'Paradise'. The man was allowed to eat anything and everything he wanted – calories don't seem to have counted in those days. However there was one condition.

Dad had the right to do anything he wanted except decide for himself what was good and what was bad. That right belonged to God alone. If God said something was good or bad, then that was to be the end of it. His word was final on the subject of good and evil.

This arrangement worked out very well at first. For instance, when God said loneliness wasn't good (Gen. 2:18) the first father could agree with that. He had tried making friends with all the different species of animal, but they had turned out to be poor conversationalists. So God went to work on making the first mother. We don't know exactly how he achieved this. All we're told is that Dad was put to sleep – the first general anaesthetic in human history – and that when he came round he seemed to be missing a rib. But the results were well worth it.

From that piece of bone God achieved the sort of reconstruction surgery plastic surgeons and scientists can only dream about. *Jurassic Park* eat your heart out! Picture the scene as, recovering from the effects of the general anaesthetic in a private ward, Dad receives his first visitor of the day. No, it's not Fido the dog or Panda the black-and-white hamster. It's ... it's ... What is it?

'Great Scott! *This is it!*'[2] Dad exclaimed before going into a swoon. No post-operative depression that day. God had done the impossible. Taking a surplus piece of the man he had made something even better. This was another perfect example of how much God loved and cared for him. Dad was on 'cloud nine'.

The unsafeway

Maybe the story would have ended happily ever after at that point if it hadn't been for an unforgettable shopping day. Once Dad got used to having Mum around he soon found a place for her. She would be good at cooking and doing the shopping. Meanwhile he could get on with the gardening. He liked doing that. Division of labour seemed a good idea at the time.

But if only he had gone shopping with his wife that day things might have turned out very differently indeed. It all happened over by the fruit counter. Mum was collecting the usual provisions for the evening meal when a shop assistant came up to her. At least that's who she thought he was. It turned out that he was actually 'Slippery Sid', who later became the patron saint of all rogue car salesmen. Sid was very good at his job – which was to sell things. He struck up a conversation with the unsuspecting shopper. This was when Mum should have realised something was wrong. The best that snakes had managed up to this point was a hiss; they had not been given the power of speech by God. This creature was quite literally speaking with a forked tongue, and what it had to say should have convinced her that she was being tricked.

One thing led to another. Before Mum knew what had happened Slippery Sid had sold her a packet of lies neatly wrapped up in a covering of half-truths. She bought it: the whole story. If only she had read the warning on the label before taking it to the check-out . . . if only her husband had been there to stop her from buying this snake's clever story . . . if only . . . But the product looked so innocent, so desirable. How could a little bit of it hurt? But it did. It hurt their friendship with God and fellowship with one another, and sowed the seeds of family breakdown in their home.

The rest, as they say, is history. The decision of the first parents to do it their way instead of God's caused trouble in their marriage, rebellion in their children and disaster to the rest of the human race. The reason can be explained using a simple illustration from nature: 'A person will reap exactly what he sows' (Gal. 6:7).

I recently found a marvellous example of this in our garden. I love gardening, but our present garden is small and the soil poor. Over the past two or three years I have been trying to do something about this. All our vegetable skins, orange peel, tea leaves, grass cuttings and other biodegradable rubbish goes into a compost tumbler. This works wonders (if you don't mind the smell). Four weeks later the result is rich compost which gets put on the garden regularly.

Like the first dad I believe in division of labour too, so when it was ready for use recently I was happy to let Barbara finish spreading it around the borders. A few weeks later I went out to do some watering. To my amazement there in one of the flower borders was a strong healthy potato plant. 'Where on earth did that come from?' I wondered.

Sixty years ago the place our house is built on was a potato farm, but I didn't think it could have come from there! All sorts of rubbish rains down into our garden during the week, but I couldn't remember it raining seed potatoes before. We don't grow vegetables so we couldn't have put it there. Then I remembered the compost bin. One of the discarded potato ends must have seeded itself when it had been dug in to the garden with the rest of our compost. Sowing and reaping; it's even a law that applies to rubbish.

The first Dad and Mum were perfect parents; but they made a big mistake. They allowed lies, deceit and half-truths to take God's place. The result was mistrust of one another, rivalry between their children and a harvest that caused the death of their eldest son.

The Bible has this story at the heart of its opening message for a very good reason. It points us directly towards the same home truth Jesus focused on when he was preparing his friends for his last day: 'If you love me, do what I tell you.'

Jesus knew what he was talking about when he told his closest friends that his teaching was to be obeyed. He'd seen the result of the first parents' ignoring of God's advice. He'd watched the horrible consequences of this all down human history, and he'd come into the world to put a stop to the world's sliding into moral chaos. He spent his life on the cross to buy a way back to the Father and the sort of home life that he'd planned for us from the very beginning.

He has a passion for our family life: a passion that it will be open to his love, and built on his truths. When this happens, then we shall find that even what was once 'rubbish' can be transformed into something beautiful by him. In the next chapter we'll see what this can mean when applied to something which has so often been reduced to the level of rubbish, but upon which family life depends for its survival: good sex.

3

GOOD SEX

The Hebrew words for man, *ish*, and woman, *ishishah* suggest a relationship which is intimate and whole. By virtue of her creation, woman is taken from within man and man belongs within woman. It wouldn't have taken the first parents long to work out how they both fitted together again. The very design of their different bodies belonged in a union as close as a sword in its sheath.

This sounds like rather graphic stuff. It is. The Bible is not coy about sex. Indeed it appears on the first page. It makes it clear that good sex was invented long before human beings found a way to spoil it. The land could not 'produce vegetation: seed-bearing plants and trees on the land that bear fruit with seed in it' (Gen. 1:11) unless the sexual process of pollination took place. The birds and the sea creatures were commanded by God to have sex (Gen. 1:2–23) and have been at it ever since!

Human beings were included in this command to 'go forth and multiply'. Our sexual urge does not come from our genes, or evolution, or animal-type lust. It is a God-created desire which he has called good and wants to bless us with.

The sad truth is that our society is getting close to changing sex from a blessing into a curse. It has turned something beautiful into something ugly and obscene. Sex is good. Sex can be great. But sex is not the same thing as Paradise. To walk into some newsagents you would think it was. The naked bodies of women and men invite us to reach up and touch with our hands, explore with our eyes, feel with our emotions and fantasise about with our minds. Instant pleasure is on offer with change from a fiver. No wonder so many people get hooked.

Sex is a modern-day god that is invading our homes. It comes in magazines, on television, through explicit videos and now down our phone lines by computer. Sex demands our attention from the selling of Levi button-fly jeans, to the soft-soap sagas that move in and out of actors' bedrooms. Sex promises Paradise to a society that has lost it. However, the horizon it offers is just a cruel image.

We can do something about this. Bringing Christ into our homes can help to change sex today from being a god into being good.

The right exposure

In the summer of 1979 Barbara and I climbed Snowdon in North Wales. The conditions were perfect: clear blue skies and uninterrupted views. I'd do it again; but I'd make sure this time we had proper walking boots rather than just stout shoes.

The route we took along the Miner's track and then up the Pyg track was both terrifying and breathtaking. At one point there was a thousand-foot drop to the left of us. One wrong move and we would have joined the fish in the corrie lake below. When we at last reached the top I finished the film off in my camera, taking in the view. It was truly spectacular – Anglesey and the coast of Ireland to the west; Merseyside, Southport and the mountains of Cumbria to the north; the Pennines and Peak District to the east. I managed to film the complete panorama by placing the camera on a rock, pressing the shutter and then moving it round by degrees.

When we got home I couldn't wait to get the pictures back. I tore open the envelope containing the slides and began to study the results. Blank. Blank. Blank. All the pictures were blank. I couldn't believe it. What had happened? Inside the slide box there was a printed note. It read something like this: 'These slides have been processed to the highest standard of manufacture. Unfortunately they have not been exposed. We suggest you examine your camera for a fault.' My heart sank. The developing firm turned out to be right. The winding mechanism of the camera had jammed. What a terrible disappointment this was. All that way and yet nothing to show for it; the film had not been exposed.

To achieve good sex in our homes and families we need to expose our minds and hearts to Christ's light. We need to open up the whole of our lives to his truth. That includes our sexuality.

This may not be easy. Some of us have grown up with a lot of wrong ideas about sex which we have learnt along the way. We may have learnt that sex was dirty, something secret and rude not to be talked about in public. On the other hand, we may have learnt that sex meant pleasure: the thrill of masturbation, the ecstasy of orgasm. Maybe we even experimented sexually with other people.

When I was teenager sex scared me to death. I was so afraid of the feelings that came with sexual arousal that I asked God to take them away. That's one prayer I'm glad he didn't answer! It was many years before I came to see sex in a positive light. God's truth on the subject can help us overcome damaged pasts.

Let me tell you about Karl. He was in his mid-twenties, happily married to a beautiful wife and they had three delightful children.

When he first came to see me Karl couldn't even bring himself to look me in the eyes. Despite the obvious joy in his home and his clear faith in Christ, Karl was haunted by the wrong sort of exposure to sex in his past. It took him a long time before he was able to talk to me about it. He had deep feelings of guilt and shame.

Karl's story began innocently enough. It was Saturday morning. His parents had gone out shopping with his elder brother and had left him at home under the watchful eye of a good neighbour. The promise of some extra pocket money had persuaded him to cut the grass while his parents were gone. After he had finished the job he went to put the lawn-mower away in the garden shed. As he did so, he accidentally knocked over a pile of old newspapers which stood in one corner.

A glossy magazine that had been wedged inside fell to the ground.

Karl picked it up. He couldn't tell from the cover what was inside, but as he turned the pages he found himself becoming breathless. His heart pounded and his head began to swim. The magazine contained graphic pictures of two men and a woman having sex. The photographer had left nothing to the imagination. Karl described the confusing feelings of disgust and fascination he had felt as he gazed at the magazine. Fascination, because this was his first introduction to sex education. Up till then, apart from the occasional conversation in the playground, Karl knew virtually nothing about the so-called 'facts of life'. His disgust came from being exposed to the human body in a way he was quite unprepared for. He had never seen an adult naked, not even his parents. To see two men and a woman in a highly aroused sexual state, doing things to each other that should never be seen in public was a terrifying experience for him. Unable to cope with what he saw, Karl hurriedly buried the magazine and ran to the toilet where he was violently sick.

Karl was just ten years old when this happened. The effect on his emotional development was catastrophic. His hormones were already awakening strange sensations within him as he had begun puberty at an early age. This over-exposure to sexual stimulation stirred feelings that a child of his age could not come to terms with. He was too scared to tell anyone what he had seen and, despite his sense of disgust, returned to this and other literature he found hidden away, again and again.

In less than five seconds Karl had been robbed of his innocence. As we talked together it was clear to me that he had mentally blanked off whole areas of his life as a result of this experience. He was unable to talk about or make sense of his sexual feelings as a grown man and repressed these under layers and layers of guilt. It was as if he had made the jump from childhood to adulthood without the process of adolescence.

Although I have altered names, places and details to protect the identity of the person concerned, this is a true story. And I do not believe it is a rare one. Karl was a victim of what we

might call 'third-party sexual abuse'. He hadn't been sexually
abused in person, but the sort of literature he was exposed to had
violated his innocence in a serious way. Talking to him and
seeing the effect that this incident had had on his life gave new
meaning for me to Jesus's words: 'But I tell you that if anyone
looks at a woman and wants to sin sexually with her, then he has
already done that sin with the woman in his mind,' (Matt. 5:28).[1]

The wrong sort of exposure to sex in Karl's life was like the
film jamming in my camera on the top of Snowdon. Karl's
emotional development had got stuck in the past and his understanding of sex in the context of love had not developed. As we
talked, wept and prayed together Christ came into this room in
his life and began to unravel the mess. Jesus is changing Karl's
sex life for good; he wants to do the same for each one of us.

Good sex?

It is essential that we teach our children good things about sex.
If we don't, someone else will do the job for us. Our children
will hear about sex from their friends in the playground. They
will watch it on television, video or computer. They will hear
about it in classes at school. They will come across it in books.
We can redress the balance by making sure that our families are
a place of healthy sexual development.

This is crucial if we are serious about bringing Christ into our
homes. In 1994 the results of an excellent national survey, *Sexual
Behaviour in Britain*, were published by Penguin Books. Two of
its findings are worth quoting here.

1   *Experience of sexual intercourse*

The report states that in the last forty years the average age at
which people first have sex has fallen dramatically. Four decades
ago the average age at which women first had sex was twenty-
one. The survey revealed that today this average has fallen by
nearly 20 per cent. Women now normally have sex for the first

time at the age of seventeen. Over the same period of time, the average age for men has come down from twenty to seventeen.[2]

The same trend can be seen in terms of first sexual experience (excluding intercourse). This has dropped from sixteen to fourteen for women and from fifteen to thirteen for men.[3]

On paper this may not seem a very large change, but the figures show an alarming trend. Forty years ago most people waited until they were adults before having sex; now most men and women have sexual intercourse before they even leave school. If this trend continues, by the end of the next generation most people will have had their first sexual experience before leaving junior school and intercourse before they've taken their GCSEs! We should be alarmed at these findings and seek to understand the reasons for these changes in our society.

The authors of this report draw two very interesting conclusions. The first is that earlier maturation of women cannot explain the changes; girls are menstruating at an earlier age but this factor cannot explain the steep decline in the age of intercourse. The second and most telling conclusion is that the changes in sexual behaviour cannot be explained by the period of the 'swinging sixties'. Although the decline in age did gather pace during the 1960s, the trend began at least a decade earlier.

The fall in the age of menstruation is not on a scale sufficient to explain the scale of the changes in age at first intercourse ... the steepest decline (in the age of first sex) occurred during the 1950s ... These data provide no evidence of a sexual revolution co-terminous with the decade of the 1960s; the major changes seem to have occurred in the previous decade.[4]

As Christians we need to look to spiritual explanations for what has been happening in Britain since the end of the Second World War. We may have successfully fought off invasion by a foreign army, but while our backs have been turned there has been another sort of invasion altogether.

Bringing Christ back into the centre of our sexual lives is the only hope for victory in this battle against the forces of darkness in our land. If you have a statistical mind, buy the book or order it from the library. It makes sobering reading.

2   *Premarital sex*

According to the report, 'sex before marriage is now nearly universal'.[5] Only 8.2 per cent of men and 10.8 per cent of women thought sex before marriage was 'always or mostly wrong'.[6]

Those of us who prepare people for Christian marriage aren't surprised by this statistic. Most of the couples who come to me to be married are either living together or have already had sex. We recently had to change our marriage preparation course because the session about 'first sex' for those who (frankly) had been doing it for years was a bit of a joke. We now try to talk about the subject in a more general way. What a tragedy.

One author, quoting counsellor Walter Trobisch, has summed up what over 90 per cent of homes and families seem to be missing in Britain today:

'We have been married for fifteen years . . .' one couple told Walter Trobisch. 'Our marriage and our family are very happy.' They recalled that with their pastor's help they had decided to save sexual intimacy for marriage. On their wedding night they saw each other naked for the first time and began to discover together the whole spectrum of tenderness and sexuality. This couple's approach is well illustrated by a figure of speech that is common in India and Africa. At their marriage this couple put a relatively cold pot on the marriage fire and found that from year to year the contents became hotter. Some Indians and Africans note that in Europe and America, when people marry they often take a boiling pot off the fire and put it in the ashes, so that it becomes colder and colder as time passes.[7]

We need to be awake to what is happening to our nation and our homes in Britain today. Much of what passes for 'good sex' is not good at all. It is sex without God, sex without responsibility, sex without love.

There are a few crumbs of comfort in the report. For example, four out of five people questioned believed extra-marital sex (adultery) was nearly always wrong. Almost as many disapproved of sex without any form of commitment.[8] This is something for us to build on. But we need to bring Christ into the debate. We need to seek his life-style for us, our families and our nation. 'Then you will know the truth, and the truth will set you free,' Jesus said (John 8:32). The trend in our society today is to be set free from anything that stops us from having sex. More and more people want it at younger and younger ages. So-called 'safe sex' is available to everyone, even children who've only just left junior school.[9] Christ did not come into the world to set us free for sex; he came to set our sex lives – and every other area of our lives – free from sin. When he does this, sex can become the most incredible making love experience in the universe. It is a wonderful way for two people to express their love for one another. But it must always be exclusive and faithful. There are no exceptions in the Bible. To learn more about God's idea of good sex see Genesis 2:23, Matthew 5:31–32, 19:3–9, Mark 10:2–12, 1 Corinthians 6:9–20, 7:1–39, and Song of Songs.

Setting an example

Barbara and I decided to wait for sex until 7 April 1979. Our wedding day. It wasn't easy. We were tempted, several times. I remember one occasion in particular when we'd been much too close to the limit we had set ourselves. Once you go past the marker it's always more difficult to go back. We gave ourselves a simple rule: no undressing or undoing anything! However, avoiding bare flesh can be very difficult, especially on hot days. My advice to our children will probably be 'Avoid all cracks, openings and bumps and you'll probably be all right!' In order to help us keep our sexual urges under control we need to make sure we get two things straight in our minds.

1   *The facts*

Marriage is one of the most stressful experiences in life. Having sex for the first time the same day as your wedding is not likely to be ecstatic bliss. In the national survey mentioned above more than 99 per cent of those questioned remembered their first experience of sexual intercourse.[10] Perhaps with good reason! I certainly remember my wedding night sixteen years ago; it was truly memorable.

After the marriage service and reception in Cheltenham, a friend took us to Great Malvern, which was about thirty miles away. A very generous family had loaned us their home for the night so that we could avoid travelling too far on our wedding day. This was especially welcome as we would have a long journey to the Lake District the next day.

We arrived in Malvern at about 5.30 p.m., and for the next hour or so neither of us could move. With the help of some college friends we had planned and prepared the reception ourselves, and by this stage we were shattered. All I can recall of those first moments on our own was drinking one cup of tea after another. I think I got through nearly fifteen. Our wedding night can be summed up like this, 'Ouch! That hurts', and 'What a messy business'.

Sixteen years later I still feel I have a lot to learn. As the psalmist says (Ps. 139:14), we are wonderfully made by God; there's a lot more to our bodies than just geography and plumbing.

As far as sex is concerned, ignorance is definitely not bliss. Christ came to bring us life in all its richness and variety and fullness (John 10:10). This includes our sex life. But good sex does not happen automatically. We need consciously to make the effort to bring Christ into our sex lives. Let me explain.

Above my desk is a reproduction of Holman Hunt's picture, *The Light of the World*, a favourite visual aid of mine. If you don't know the picture, it shows the risen Christ holding a lantern, standing outside a door and knocking. There are all sorts of weeds and plants growing up in front of the door and no handle on the outside of it. The only way the door can be opened is by the person inside the house.

The text beneath the painting is from Revelation 3:20, 'Here I am! I stand at the door and knock. If anyone hears my voice and opens the door, I will come in and eat with him, and he with me.'

These words remind us of what we thought about in chapter 2, when we looked together at John 14:23. Jesus does not barge his way into any part of our lives; he waits outside to be asked to come in. Christ's entry into our sex lives is via the same route. He wants to be part of this most intimate of places in our homes, but he comes in by invitation only.

On our wedding night before we shut the bedroom door, we went down on our knees and asked Christ into this special room of our lives. You may think this sounds 'super-spiritual' or pious ... or even mad. But for me it was a conscious decision to let Jesus be head of our bed as well as our home. By giving him access to the most intimate place in our family life, we can help to establish a Christ-centred pattern of sexual experience. Looking back, my only regret is that I haven't let Christ into more of it as my marriage has progressed. The best way to ensure that our bedrooms are places where sex is really good is to give Christ his rightful place in our passions as well as our prayers.

2   Our fears

Fear can make us do strange things. When we moved to London in 1990, we wondered whether our home would continue to be the safe place it had been in Cumbria. Our new home was fitted with a burglar alarm, and this was new to us. Although burglaries did happen in Cumbria, there was a much greater sense of trust between neigbours.

Things are very different in London. On our first night in the house we reluctantly set the alarm when we went to bed. To our dismay it went off half an hour after we were asleep. I woke up and crept down the stairs, expecting to be met by burglars. But it was a false alarm.

In those first few weeks the alarm went off several times during the night for no apparent reason. 'Surely by now the burglar has got the message,' I thought as I checked the windows at 2 a.m. for the umpteenth time.

Then one evening as we were watching television I noticed the 'sensor eye' in the corner of the ceiling switch on and off, indicating that the security beam had been interrupted. Yet no one was moving about in the room; Barbara and I were both sitting still, watching television.

Then something happened which made me realise what might be causing the alarm to trigger. The fireplace was directly in line with the electronic eye. When the coal burnt down to a certain level, it suddenly dropped in the grate. There was enough movement in this to disturb the beam and activate the alarm. We had discovered the cause of our frequent alarm calls during the night. Burglars were not responsible after all.

The idea of asking, and then allowing Christ into our sex lives may fill us with fear. The idea of his presence in this area of our lives may set off alarm bells every time we think about it. These may be the result of a guilty conscience. Perhaps there are sexual sins in our past, such as pre-marital sex, which we prefer to forget about or to hide from him. We may be afraid because we don't know what he will do or say to us once we face him with these past sins.

Or we may live with bad memories from childhood. Our parents may have told us off when they found us masturbating, leaving us with the idea that if we wanted sex then we needed to be secretive about it. We may have been taught that 'sex' is a dirty word which we shouldn't use and anything to do with it is dirty too. On the other hand, we may have been told nothing at all. In any event, we may have grown up without positive and loving guidance from someone in our lives whom we loved and respected. Therefore when it comes to our relationship to Christ, we find sex a hard subject to talk to him about.

This attitude is rather ridiculous when you think about it. You may not think much of your body when you stand in front of a mirror and look. But the human form is the closest any of us will get here on earth to seeing God. When God became man in the person of Jesus Christ, he left nothing out. His human form revealed God perfectly to the world. I realise this is difficult territory for many of us. We may fear that to talk of God in human terms such as this somehow belittles him and puts him on our level. The truth is that all human beings are made in the image and likeness of the one who is fully and completely *the* image of God (see Gen. 1:27; Col. 1:15–16). One author puts it like this:

In the case of sex we need to begin with a right understanding of our bodies. We need to be able to 'see' in nakedness what God intended us to see in it: the glory of His presence in the world, the highest expression of what He Himself looks like, the very form He assumed when he visited the earth in person. Can we not detect His Own paint still wet on our skins, and the marks of His fingers imprinted in our ears, in our eye sockets, on our lips and on our genitals? Only when we perceive that nakedness is as close as most of us will ever get to seeing God in the flesh, that these poor bodies of ours are the natural (as opposed to supernatural) expression of God's glory, only then can we begin to understand also that sex is the closest thing to touching Him: the closest, that is, next to the Eucharist itself.[11]

We do not need to be afraid about bringing Christ into our sex lives. He made the penis, gave it the capacity to erect, ejaculate and produce some of the most intense feelings of pleasure known to man. He made the vagina. He invented the 'G-spot' – not sex therapists. He was the one who designed the female form so that a woman can experience the heights and depths of orgasm during sex.

I wish to cause no offence by stating this. But I believe these truly are the facts of life that we need to learn in our homes and teach (at appropriate times) to our children. If as parents and partners we learn to bring God into our sexuality in a Christ-

centred way, then we will be teaching our children by example
something they can never learn anywhere else.

If we teach them that Christ, not man, created sex they are far
more likely to go to him when they get into trouble. When sex
brings us to our knees, we shall find there someone who has been
through all this before us. And with his love, we can make our
secret bedroom-places a sacred place for him.

With all your mind

Letting Christ into our sex lives means opening up our minds to
him. For some of us this may require sexual therapy or counselling. For most of us it will simply mean doing the necessary
homework. Give yourself the following test. Put a tick by the
subjects you think the Bible says something specific:

1	Marriage __	12	Sex therapy __
2	Polygamy __	13	Oral sex __
3	Virginity __	14	Same-sex love __
4	The sex organs __	15	Adultery __
5	Nudity __	16	Masturbation __
6	Coitus interruptus __	17	Contraception __
7	Homosexual sex __	18	Rape __
8	Pre-marital sex __	19	Pornography __
9	Surrogate parenthood __	20	Prostitution __
10	Single parenting __	21	Bestiality __
11	Sex techniques and positions __	22	Voyeurism __

Now turn to Appendix A for the answers. You may be surprised at what a lot the Bible has to say and at what it doesn't
say. One of the ways we can love God with all our minds is to let
him clean the rubbish out. Some of the teaching about sex we
have grown up with or heard in Christian circles comes from
tradition and not Scripture. By doing our homework from the
Word of God we can help to grow healthy sexual appetites and
attitudes.

> Therefore I urge you ... to offer your bodies as living
> sacrifices, holy and pleasing to God – which is your spiritual
> worship. Do not conform any longer to the pattern of this
> world, but be transformed by the renewing of your mind.
> Then you will be able to test and approve what God's will is –
> his good, pleasing and perfect will (Rom. 12:1–2).

Putting Paul's teaching into practice means being ready to make
some changes. From time to time I go for a walk around my
bookshelves. I imagine that Jesus is looking over my shoulder
and I ask him to show me what doesn't belong there. I am
particularly sensitive about this because I know my children can
come into my study when I am out and take books without me
knowing. I want to be sure that the sort of information available
to them will build them up into godly people. That includes
godly attitudes and understanding about sex.

Try having a stock-take in your home today. Perhaps this will
mean a visit to the garden shed (or your equivalent) if there are
things there a child should never see. However carefully you hide
things, children have an uncanny knack of finding them. On the
other hand, you may need to visit a bookshop if you find you
don't have anything worth reading on the subject of sex.

The same sort of action needs to be taken in our television
room. If we have our own video collection, we need to ask Christ
to help us weed out films or programmes that displease him and
add some that don't. If you're not sure how this can be done, ask
yourself whether you would be comfortable watching a particular
video with a minister, church elder or your mother-in-law
present! If in doubt, dump it. This is what Jesus meant when he
said: 'If your right eye causes you to sin, gouge it out and throw
it away. It is better for you to lose one part of your body than for
your whole body to go into hell' (Matt. 5:29).

The same principle applies to television in general. Those of
us with cable, satellite or some other sort of hi-tech machine
need to be especially careful here. We need to do all that we can
to guard our minds and those of our children from the invasion
of obscene or dubious material. If in doubt about a programme,

be ruthless and switch it off. The consequences for you and your
home if you don't could be very far-reaching indeed:

> Things that cause people to sin are bound to come, but woe to
> that person through whom they come. It would be better for
> him to be thrown into the sea with a millstone tied around his
> neck than for him to cause one of these little ones to sin. So
> watch yourselves (Luke 17:1–2).

This was Jesus speaking to his disciples: not to pagans. If we
take his words seriously, we must take responsibility for protect-
ing our homes. I find far too many Christian families where this
does not take place. 'Watch yourselves,' Jesus said. Perhaps we
should put this motto above our television screens to remind us
every time we switch on.

Talk about it

Many parents find it difficult to talk to their children about sex.
This is understandable. It is an intimate subject which affects our
human emotions very deeply. It may be that our parents talked
to us about sex in a natural way and this made them easy to talk
to about sex. If so then we shall find it a lot more 'natural' to
bring up the subject with our own children. On the other hand,
it is more likely that our parents may have been unwilling or too
embarrassed to discuss sex with us. Research by Dr Miriam
Stoppard has shown that this is a very common problem which
young people experience as they grow up and it can have a
profound effect on how their attitudes to sex develop. In her
conversations with children she says this:

> One of the things that you complained about was that your
> parents seemed to leave the initiative for starting a sexual
> discussion with you. You felt that your parents were thinking
> 'Well if she wants to know something she can always come to
> me.' Or, 'If he wants to ask anything about sex he will.' While
> on the one hand a few of you thought this showed your

parents' respect for your privacy most of you thought that it
showed your parents' discomfort at discussing the subject of
sex openly. You took this discomfort as an unwillingness on
the part of your parents to talk about sex and therefore found
it difficult to raise the subject yourself.[12]

Her advice to parents in the light of this is simple and direct: as
parents we need to start as we mean to go on.

Nearly every parent I spoke to said that open communication
between parents and children had to start when children were
young. If they weren't talking freely [about sex] when their
children reached adolescence then the difficulties both the
parents and the children were experiencing made it almost
impossible to start.[13]

When it comes to talking to our children about sex, Barbara and
I have had success and failure. One of our children has always
raised the subject with us in a natural, matter of fact sort of way
(sometimes at the most inconvenient moments); one of them has
not wanted to talk about the subject at all, and the other two fall
somewhere between the two extremes. This came home to me
very forcibly when Barbara was due to go to the Family Planning
Clinic recently. The Clinic on this occasion happened to be
taking place in the early evening. The children know that Mum
doesn't usually go out on her own in the evening unless it is to a
meeting, and in any case she usually lets them know in advance
about this. Elliott (aged eleven) was curious. 'Where are you
going Mum?' he asked. 'Don't be so nosey!' I said. At that
particular moment I was trying to get cleared up and ready for a
church meeting and didn't relish the idea of a family planning
discussion. I could tell by the way he asked the question that he
wasn't going to leave it at that. However, Barbara (the more
sensible of Elliott's two parents) simply answered his question:
'I'm going to the clinic,' she said. Now for some children that
would be enough: but not Elliott. I am sure that when he grows
up, he is either going to be a world famous detective or else a

brain surgeon! 'Why are you going to the clinic, Mum? Aren't you very well?' he continued, undeterred by the black looks I was giving him. 'No, I'm fine. I'm just going to get some condoms,' Barbara went on.

This was all the encouragement Elliott needed. He proceeded to launch into a full-scale enquiry about his parents' family planning philosophy and practice. Before long one of his older brothers and his sister had both joined in the inquest. Here are some of the questions that they asked between them on this occasion:

'Why do you use condoms, Mum? Don't you like having babies any more?'

'Where does the sperm go in the condom? How does it work?'

'What happens if you don't use a condom?'

'You need to use tampons when you go swimming sometimes, don't you?'

'Does it hurt when you put those things inside you?'

'Where does the blood come from?'

'You know you're supposed to check your breasts every month, Mum; it says so in Dad's book.'

On an occasion like this it was difficult to stop them asking questions and it gave us an excellent opportunity to let them discuss sex with us openly and without embarrassment. I couldn't help noticing that one of the children was conspicuously absent when all this sex talk was going on; but I am certain he was listening from his bedroom with the door open! We have always taken the line that children should not be pressurised into talking about sex if they don't want to, but have tried to encourage them to talk when the opportunity comes up. For some children who (like the boy eavesdropping from his bedroom) find sex talk rather difficult, we may need to take the initiative as parents. One way we can do this is to read books about sex with them.

Getting started

When they were around five to seven years old we found one book in particular a very good starting point for talking about things: *Who made me?* by M. and M. Doney. I have listed some other materials in Appendix B which are available from a local library or book shop and have commented on those which I have found to be particularly useful. The most important thing is to answer our children's questions as honestly as we can, without telling them more than their questions require. We also need to tailor our answers to their level of understanding. This varies from child to child and as parents we know our children's temperament best and can be guided by this in our conversations with them. We need to be aware, however, that if we leave it too late to talk to them about things like menstruation, masturbation and other topics they may be concerned about, we shall rob them of information they need in order to make wise choices. I recently approached a school nurse about this. She suggested a number of practical methods that she used in her work with school-children and I have included some of her ideas in Appendixes C and D. I particularly liked the Word Search and Puberty Quiz that she uses to help children get used to using sex words. As parents this can be particularly useful if we have grown up believing that such words are 'naughty' and are not comfortable in using them ourselves.

One author (Lynda Madaras) has taken this 'word-shy' problem a stage further by advocating that sex education should include talking to children about slang sex words with which they are familiar but may not necessarily understand. I cannot go along with all that she says about this but I think she makes an important point. We do need to be aware of what sex words are being used by the culture our children live in – if only to answer their frank questions about expressions such as 'blow-job', 'wanking', or 'getting laid'. We may need their help in identifying some of these everyday words and will probably find using them rather embarrassing at first. If we are serious about talking to them about sex, however, we need to be aware of the language of sex too. By discussing slang words and what they really mean we might save them from finding out the hard way or the wrong way what certain slang words mean.

As seen on TV

Advertising has made some aspects of sex talk easier for us as parents. For instance, we now see tampons and other sanitary products regularly advertised on television. If, like me, you cringe inside when these adverts are run and say to yourself: 'Must we have this sort of thing displayed in our living room when we're in the middle of eating tea?' I have often walked out of the room at this point or pressed the 'sound off' button on the remote control. Yet this does provide a way of introducing a subject to our children in a non-threatening way. This can be especially important if you are a single father trying to bring up a daughter.

It may not be very wise to turn the television off there and then and launch into a deep discussion about feminine hygiene; I'd probably get lynched in our home if I tried to do this during an exciting episode of *The New Adventures of Superman*, for instance. But when the programme you are all watching is over and you are doing the clearing up together, here is an opportunity for us as parents to raise the matter over the kitchen sink. We might ask questions like, 'Do you know what that tampons advert was about?' or 'Why do women have to buy those special pads that they advertised on television just now?' as a way of helping open up the subject. One parent told me that talking to her daughter in this sort of ordinary matter of fact way had helped her to accept menstruation as just another part of life. Indeed, she told her mum that she was going to wear a sanitary towel the next day when she went to school, just to see what it was going to be like when the real event happened. This seemed to me to be a healthy attitude for a twelve-year-old to have. Treating sexual matters in an ordinary way with our children will help them to handle their sexual development without unnecessary hang-ups.

In chapter 2 of *The Hiding Place*, Corrie Ten Boom tells of a train journey she once made with her father. As they travelled in their compartment together she asked her father what 'sex sin' was. Her father made no reply, but as they came into the station where they were due to disembark he took one of their large suitcases off the luggage rack and asked Corrie to carry it. As he picked up the rest of their belongings, it soon became clear that Corrie was quite unable to move the case. Her father was well aware of this and wisely told her that 'sex sin' was like this heavy suitcase; it was too heavy a burden for her to understand at her age.

This story illustrates very well the principle which Jesus taught concerning our treatment of children: If anyone causes one of these little ones who believe in me to sin, it would be better for him to have a large millstone hung around his neck and to be drowned in the depths of the sea (Matt. 18:6).

Corrie's father knew she was not old enough to understand about sexual sins and therefore preferred to leave the question unanswered. In our sex talk with our children we too need to be wary of exposing them to sexual information which they are not mature enough to handle. Let us always answer our children's sex questions honestly, but have the wisdom to tell them enough but no more than they need to know or are able to cope with at any particular point in their development. In practice this means keeping the lines of communication with them constantly open, doing the necessary homework on sex education ourselves and guarding their minds and hearts day by day in our prayers as they are exposed to influences and ideas which are outside our control . . . but not God's.

'Get wisdom, get understanding; do not forget my words or swerve from them. Do not forsake wisdom and she will protect you; love her, and she will watch over you. Wisdom is supreme; therefore get wisdom. Though it cost you all you have, get understanding.' (Prov. 4:5–8)

I have spent a lot of time in this chapter talking about parents and sex rather than sex education for families. The reason is that good, Christ-centred sexual habits between ourselves will lead to good sexual habits in our homes and families. This brings us back to the spiritual principle in Galatians 6:7–9: – we shall reap what we sow.

This needn't make us feel ashamed if we have made mistakes in the past. Christ comes into our sex lives to cleanse and make them whole, not to punish and shame us. There's quite enough of this happening in our guilty consciences without the need for him to add further accusation (see Rom. 2:15; 1 Pet. 3:16; cf. John 8:9). The wonderful message of the gospel is that Christ came to save us from our sin. That was the whole point of what he said through St John to the Christians in the church at Laodicea (Rev. 3:20). Their Christian lives had become polluted, and he was offering them a way out of their sickening spiritual mediocrity.

Let me sum up with the following illustration. I recently visited W. H. Smith to look for some books on sex that I could recommend to other people. I felt rather self-conscious looking through them, especially the ones with explicit pictures.

The particular book I was looking for wasn't on the shelf, so I went around the other side of the bookcase to see if it had been placed there by accident. I had to smile when I saw what was there. Directly behind the books on sex was a row of Bibles.

I realised as I stood there smiling to myself that here was the answer. To have good sex in our homes we need the Bible in one hand and some good books about sex in the other. Some books on sex should be put straight into our dustbin; some we should read and then throw away; some (suitable for the age group concerned) we should buy and read *with* our children – don't give the book to them and say, 'Here, read this'; one or two really good adult ones we should keep on the top shelf far out of reach of young curious fingers and use when we need reminding how sex is meant to work.

And the Bible? We never need to put that book in the bin or tear pages out of it, or put it out of reach of the children. This is the best 'good sex' guide we shall ever possess. As we use it day by day our sex lives will be transformed. Praise God! We are wonderfully and fearfully made. 'Awesome!', as my children would put it.

4

GOD'S FAMILY PLAN

My sex education consisted of a double period of biology in the first year at secondary school. I remember it well. A young female teacher did her best to draw diagrams on the blackboard and answer pupils' questions. She was bright red in the face for most of the lesson, and few of us took the matter very seriously. Twenty-seven years later AIDS has changed all that.

Today, sex education is a serious issue because more and more young people's lives are at risk. The AIDS scare has brought the condom into our living rooms and made it a household name.

There is much debate in education at the moment about how sex education should be taught in schools. Thankfully the emphasis is now on committed relationships as the best place for sex to take place. The threat of people dying from sex has made our society think again about what we do and how we do it.

As we pick up our Bibles each day we have a unique privilege. In its pages we find God's blueprint for our homes and families.

Blueprints are very important. When our church was undergoing major repairs I had piles of plans in my study. The architect prepared them; the church studied and then approved them; finally, a contractor was appointed and he acted upon them. As work progressed I found it increasingly important to study these plans. There was one tricky moment when I wished I had studied them more carefully. It all happened over a piece of glass.

At the back of the church the architect proposed a glass screen. This would create a light and attractive foyer. We were all very pleased with the concept, and the builder went ahead.

By chance I picked up the drawings for the screen one day and realised the disturbing truth: the glass that was detailed in the plans was wired, not clear. There were good reasons for this. The screen needed to be fire resistant and wired glass was the cheapest way to accomplish this. But wired glass did not fit in with the original design concept. The whole point of having glass was to make it easy for people to see into the church. Wired glass would create a different impression.

This was a very tricky moment in the building project, and it created some unwelcome conflict. But it was worth it in the end. The extra cost of making the plans conform to the original design concept has been more than outweighed by the beauty of the finished result. Sticking to the design may be costly, but sometimes we need to be willing to pay for what we believe to be important. This is particularly significant when it comes to God's blueprint for families.

It is crucial to know and understand God's family plan. We need to check our family planning against it. His family plan included sex, but it didn't begin there. It began with a home which was completely 'green' and a man who was put there to look after it. Let's take another look at Genesis 2.

A place with boundaries

God planned that the human family should have definite boundaries. He created geographical and moral limits for human beings. The place name of Adam and Eve's home tells us a lot about the geography. They lived in a spot called Eden, which means 'bliss'. Their home had a greenhouse temperature without the damaging effects that go with it. The climate conditions were so good that food grew in a constant supply.

The trees were not only the source of this food supply; they were incredibly beautiful to look at, especially the two in the middle of the garden. One of these was strictly off limits: at least, its fruit was. However, God never said anything about not touching or looking at this tree. Eve got this crucial boundary fatally wrong and paid a very heavy penalty for it.

Eden was a safe and secure place to live. The animals were

tame, the food abundant, the temperature and environment ideal. God wanted to keep it that way.

He planned that this home should be somewhere human beings could be themselves. A place where they could be free to do as they liked, eat what they liked, go where they liked. A place where a man and woman could be so free that they had no need to hide anything. They could even walk about naked without worrying about what other people might think.

To keep it like this, God gave human beings specific moral boundaries within which they were to live. He didn't make the rules complicated or difficult to understand. In fact they couldn't have been simpler. Their moral freedom was limited by one cardinal rule: '. . . but you must not eat from the tree of the knowledge of good and evil, for when you eat of it you will surely die' (Gen. 2:16–17).

In practice this meant that 'good and evil' were non-negotiable. Right and wrong were to be measured by what God said, not by what people said or felt appropriate at the time. Human beings were not free to mess about with these two concepts and start playing God. They were clearly warned by God that if they disregarded this cardinal rule, it would be the beginning of the end. From what happened next in the Genesis story, we know it was.

What has happened to these two boundaries of geography and morality in family life today? God planned that the 'geography' of the family should be a home full of bliss. It should be a place where human beings have all they need to live and more besides. It should be a beautiful place to look at and to live in. This is God's Family Plan.

So take a quick look at your experience of family. Bliss? I doubt it. Maybe there are moments of bliss – 'the sitting around the tree on Christmas Day' bliss; the 'fixing the washing machine without having to call out a plumber this time' bliss; the 'sitting by the log fire with a cup of tea, your feet up and the children all safely tucked up in bed' bliss; the 'swishing on skis down a mountain slope covered with virgin snow and no tourists' bliss; the 'overwhelming sense of ecstatic emotion flooding over you

during simultaneous orgasm' bliss; the 'holding your first child
in your arms after all the mess and medical people have gone out
of the room at last' bliss. Come to think of it, maybe there's
more bliss in our families than we first imagine.

But how long does the bliss last? Waiting for our first child to
be born was unbearable. Barbara's contractions began in the
early hours of Sunday morning when she was at home in bed.
When they got more frequent we called the hospital. Eventually,
by Monday morning it was time for her to go in. Contractions
were stop-start, stop-start, and poor Barbara was exhausted.

It took until quarter past four on Tuesday afternoon before
Junior decided he would at last put in an appearance. There
seemed to be nurses and doctors and plastic tubes everywhere. I
couldn't wait for them all to go so that I could savour this unique
moment, the start of our family life.

Eventually, after what seemed like hours, the three of us were
left in peace. Barbara, in a state of exhaustion, unconscious in
bed; Dad, in a state of euphoria, slouched in the chair by her
head; and the miraculous bundle of humanity called Nathaniel
safely held in my arms, having been fed.

'So this is it,' I said to myself. 'This is what it feels like to be a
dad. Wow!' I wanted that moment of bliss to last for ever. But it
didn't.

It doesn't, does it? The bliss of the Christmas tree gives way
to the present which broke the first time you used it; the bliss of
the mended washing machine gives way to the freezer's breaking
down full of food; the bliss of putting your feet up gives way to
someone upstairs being sick all over the bed; the bliss of the ski
slope gives way to the crunched cartilage; the bliss of orgasm can
give way to the mess in the bed; the bliss of childbirth gives way
to exhaustion! Bliss, bliss, bliss. At times life can be sheer bliss.
But it doesn't last.

'Count your blessings, name them one by one and it will
surprise you how much the Lord has done' the old chorus goes.
'Bless the LORD, O my soul; and all that is within me bless his
holy name. Bless the LORD, O my soul, and forget not all his
benefits,' says the psalmist (Ps. 103:1–2). We need to count our

times of bliss and make a consious effort to remember them, because they are all too short.

The normal family life is not an experience of uninterrupted bliss. Indeed so many of us get demoralised by our families that we may even feel like giving up on them altogether. 'How can what God has planned and supposed to be so good, bring so much pain and heartache?' we say to ourselves. And, at our worst moments, 'If this is God's idea of a family plan, count me out.'

My wife Barbara summed this up for me when we were talking together about a recent problem in our home. She compared family life to her experience of mountain climbing. Just when you think you've reached the top you find yourself at the bottom of the next summit! Sometimes it can feel like family life is one long uphill struggle. Worse still, just when you think you may have got to grips with one problem another begins to loom on the horizon. No wonder so many of us find ourselves starting to believe in Murphy's Law: Anything that can go wrong will go wrong.

According to Murphy's Law:
The chance of a slice of toast falling with the buttered side down is directly proportional to the cost of the carpet.
The repair man will never have seen a model quite like yours.
No matter how hard you shop for an item, after you buy it, you'll find it on sale somewhere cheaper.
The other line at the check-out always moves faster.
The light at the end of the tunnel is the headlamp of an oncoming train.

When God planned the family, he designed it to be a place of bliss. That was its geographical location: the land of bliss. This isn't daydreaming on my part. It's all there in the Bible. When we hunger for a life of bliss we are craving for something that we were made for.

Why did Jesus's preaching get such a good reaction from ordinary people? Because he struck a chord in their hearts. 'Jesus went throughout Galilee ... preaching the good news of the

kingdom ... Large crowds ... followed him' (Matt. 4:23–25).
They followed him because his life, teaching, healing and love
pointed them to the kingdom of God: a place of bliss in Israel
again – even better than the state of things when David was king.
Jesus revived hope in people who had lost it. He wants to do the
same in us as he comes into our homes to reveal to us his family
planning. Alleluia! What a Saviour.

The moral slide

God planned that the human home should be a place of moral
purity. It was to be a place of communion, in the widest sense of
that word. Communion between man and woman in their
partnership in the job of housekeeping. Communion in their
conscious decision to keep things out of their relationships that
would tear them apart. Communion in the joining of their bodies
in a way that says 'I love you' more than anything else can.
Communion in their intimate fellowship with God in their home
day by day. What's this communion like in your home at the
moment? Let me describe to you a recent experience in ours.

It was Friday teatime. Fridays are always a difficult day for us.
It's the end of the week. It's the evening before my day off.
We're all tired and wanting to relax and unwind from the
pressures of the week. The conversation at the table that night
went something like this:

Dad: OK, time to clear up. Whose turn is it to help?
A: I did it last week; I'm not doing it again.
C: No you didn't. You got out of it because you had lots of
        homework to do. It's your turn and B's.
B: Oh no. Not me. I'm not clearing up. I'm definitely not
        doing it. I had to do your jobs last night because you were
        at a friend's house. I'm not going to clear up two nights in
        a row. So there.
Dad: It's no good you all arguing about it. Someone's got to
        help. You know the drill. Two of you volunteer for tea

today and the other two do it tomorrow. Let's have some
co-operation, can we please? So then, who's it to be?
(Silence)

Dad: Well, in that case I'll decide. A and B can do it tonight and
C and D can help me do it tomorrow. That's the only way
to make it fair.
(More silence and then an outburst)

A: *No. I am not* going to do it tonight. Why can't Mum do it?

Dad: That's enough. Your mother has work to do. I'm ashamed
of all of you. Leave the table. I'll do it myself.

Not all our mealtimes are like this, I'm pleased to say. But too
many of them are. Co-operation seems to be such a hard thing
to achieve. By the time you've been through a real-life dialogue
like the one above, you feel that the moral foundations of your
family life are crumbling beneath your feet. There are moments
when Barbara and I have felt close to despair. It's like trying to
climb a steep slippery slide when you've got nothing to hold on
to except people below you.

This is what it can feel like when we look at the moral slide in
our society today and wonder where to start. The mass of
statistics produced by K. Wellings *et al.* only tell us what we
already know from looking around us: human relationships are
in a complete moral muddle and family life seems to be right in
the middle of it. When this happens we can be tempted to do
one of three things:

1 Switch the goal-posts

I am not a great lover of football. But my wife and three sons
are. This meant that television viewing during the World Cup of
1994 was football, football and more football. I gave in to peer
pressure: I was, after all, outnumbered four to one. I cannot
remember anything about the series except for one incident. It
came during the match between Bulgaria and Mexico.

Part way through the game one of the goal-posts fell down. I
was on my feet cheering. At last something really entertaining

had happened. What was really funny was the dialogue of the commentators who tried to 'talk over' the long delay. They kept talking about the most unimportant details in their attempt to fill the space. In the end, to huge applause, officials brought on a completely new goal-post.

When the goal we're aiming at seems too hard to reach, we may be tempted to switch it for another one. This was what Eve was tempted to do. The serpent offered her another goal. Instead of depending on God, she was tempted to take over God's place for him.

'Knowing good and evil' had nothing to do with academic knowledge. The Hebrew word for knowledge in this verse means 'an opening', a 'becoming acquainted with', an 'ability'.[1] The temptation which Eve gave into was the temptation to take control of moral boundaries and make up the rules for herself. Adam quickly followed suit without a word of protest, and together they dragged the whole of humanity into the snake's clever trap.

This is what happens when we abandon God's pattern for human relationships and make up something else to put in its place. There is growing pressure in our society to base the idea of 'family' on what is right in our own eyes rather than on an objective morality: 'If what I'm doing doesn't hurt anyone else, why shouldn't I do it?'; 'It works for me – surely that means it can't be wrong'; 'All that matters is that you have a stable and loving relationship with someone.'

This may sound convincing in our modern age where morality has become adrift. However it doesn't match up with what Jesus taught. He condemned the Pharisees and teachers of the law for moving the goal-posts. In his sermon on the mount he took people back to basics. 'You have heard that it was said . . . but I say to you . . .' This wasn't the start of a new religion. Jesus was restating the moral boundaries which had been intended from the dawn of human history but had been deliberately ditched.

2   Go with the flow

'If you can't beat 'em, join 'em' so the saying goes. There is no
doubt in my mind that trying to follow Christ's pattern for our
homes will bring us trouble. It may be that we are married to a
non-Christian. It may be that we have no Christian background
and are now trying to change patterns we've followed for years.
The temptation to give in and follow the crowd is a real one, and
we need to be ready for it when it comes.

I remember an occasion when we stayed with some friends
before we were married. They weren't Christians but had kindly
offered to put us up when we were passing through that town.
When we arrived they showed us to our room. It was a double
bedroom with a double bed in it; on the bed was a set of two
towels each. The message came over loud and clear – they
assumed that we would sleep together.

Barbara and I looked at each other, took a deep breath and
then I plucked up courage to tell them our problem with the
sleeping arrangements. 'Do you have any other beds I could
sleep on?' I asked. 'Barbara and I don't believe in sex before
marriage.' They took it very well, but it was hard to go against
the flow. My words sounded like bad manners. It was not easy to
question their hospitality arrangements and make them fit in
with my requirements. After all, we were only guests. How much
easier it would have been to go with the flow.

We aren't told what Eve said to Adam when she gave him the
forbidden fruit. Perhaps he thought, 'Better eat it to keep the
wife happy' or 'Looks good to me; a little bit can't do me any
harm' or 'She's eaten it and doesn't seem to be suffering any side
effects. Why shouldn't I do it too?'

As we read these verses and apply them to our own situation,
we realise the same temptations are around today, urging us to
conform to what other people do. We need to be prepared to be
different; to put up a struggle if necessary and fight for the moral
boundaries that are in the Bible but are not being followed by
those around us – even by other Christians.

Adam didn't even say one word to challenge his wife's action in giving him something God had forbidden: not even one word. At least when the snake tempted his wife she had an argument with it. Adam didn't even offer a token protest at this blatant departure from 'the garden rule' which had been given directly to him (Gen. 2:16).

'All that is required for evil to triumph is for a good man to do nothing', as the saying goes. Going with the flow takes us away from Christ and his pattern for the family. 'For wide is the gate and broad is the road that leads to destruction, and many enter through it. But small is the gate and narrow the road that leads to life, and only a few find it' (Matt. 7:13–14). When Adam opened his mouth it was to satisfy his appetite, not his Lord. The temptation for us to follow suit is one we all need to face; we have all inherited his family likeness.

3 Run away and hide

Escapism is a third possible response to the moral slide in our society. Adam and Eve chose this method when God came to look for his pattern in their lives one day. They literally ran away and hid from him (Gen. 3:8). This did seem to work for a while; however, in the end they had to face up to their own problems and allow God to help them come to terms with the consequences of their sin.

Sometimes we run away and hide from reality in the church. From our safe hiding place amongst Christians we can look out on the world and say, 'Isn't it terrible? What's going to become of it?' We can go to 'holy' conferences on the problems of AIDS or unwanted pregnancies or marriage breakdown and speculate about what we can do about these issues. We can even learn counselling skills and then practise them on other people in an attempt to satisfy our urge to 'do something'.

None of these things are bad in themselves. However they can become a convenient bush in which to hide ourselves. By running and hiding in the 'isn't this terrible' place or the 'other people's needs and problems are far more important than mine' place, or the 'I can make it on my own' place, we deny Christ access into our own lives.

Yet the way to change the climate of moral decay in our society is to let Christ begin with us. God's question to the first man and woman, 'Where are you?' is a question that all of us need to let him ask us. 'Where am I in relation to where God would like me to be?'; 'What is my family pattern and how does it match up to the one I read about in the Bible?'; 'Is my home a place of trust and partnership and absolute honesty?'; 'How much of my life is hidden away from my family and from God?'

You and I can do nothing at all to change other people, but when we come to God we can do something about allowing him to change us. We've no reason to hide anything from him because he is only interested in changing us for the good. When Christ comes into our homes he wants to bring us face to face with reality. The problems and issues you and I see in the world around us may be the very ones he wants to deal with in our lives.

I heard a story of a parish weekend once. It takes us to the heart of the matter. Here's what happened.

The church weekend away was all prepared. Parents with teenagers were going to spend three days together trying to learn how to communicate better.

The title of the opening session was 'Let's pretend'. Parents met in one room and the teenagers met in another. The leader spoke to the parents first, and set them a task. On the blackboard at the front he wrote, 'The thing I most dislike about my teenager is . . .' He explained that this was a 'free-for-all' session and there were 'no holds barred'; the parents could say and write whatever they liked.

Then he left the room and went in with the teenagers. Just like before he told them they were free to say anything. Then he wrote on their blackboard, 'The thing I most dislike about my parents is . . .'

They didn't need much prompting. They came out with all the usual things: 'They shout too much'; 'They bug me'; 'They nag me to do my homework'; 'They make me do jobs in the house'; 'They're always going on at me . . .' Meanwhile in the other room the parents had nearly filled their blackboard. Their comments were fairly predictable too: 'They're lazy'; 'They don't show me respect'; 'They answer back'; 'They smell'; 'They have annoying habits'; 'They're noisy'; 'They get on my nerves . . .'

As time went by, the adults found this was really good fun. Here at last they were able to say what really got to them about their kids. What's more, they discovered that other people had problems like theirs. This made them feel a whole lot better about their inability to cope.

Then the mood in the adults' room began to change. It happened as a woman stood up to speak. 'You know something,' she said, 'looking at what we've written has really made me think. A lot of the things up there are the sorts of things we do to our children. We get on their nerves. I'm sure we could learn to respect them a bit more – at least, I know I could. I think we've missed off the most important point of all.'

She came up to the front and wrote her suggestion on the blackboard. When everyone saw it they all agreed that this one comment said everything. They therefore decided to erase all the other statements and send for the leader to tell him they had finished.

The time came to put the two groups together. First the adults came into the teenagers' room. This was to be the moment of truth. Now was their chance to get even with mum and dad and say things they'd always wanted to. It was a difficult half hour for the parents, but they all tried to listen and learn.

Then came the adults' turn. The teenagers followed them back into their room. The blackboards had been rolled up until everyone was assembled. When the leader arrived he was curious. Where were all the comments from the parents? Had they only used a small area? Had his method failed to work for the grown-ups?

There were some sounds of amusement from some of the teenagers as they guessed that mum and dad hadn't found as many bad things as they had. But there was silence when the leader rolled down the board. On it was written the following words: 'What we most dislike about our teenagers is ... They are too much like us.'

A deep hush fell on the room as the words struck home. Tears began to flow, and all over the hall parents got together with their teenagers and began to talk. The leader didn't have to say much. The one-sentence statement had said it all. There was straight talking; there was forgiveness and there was a lot of emotional healing. Indeed that weekend there was more bliss in some of those families than there had been for a very long time.

God's family plan for you and me is simple: it's bliss, sheer bliss.

5

BABIES

Anyone who has had a baby can be forgiven for saying that the words 'bliss' and 'babies' don't always belong in the same sentence. Here are some of the things people said to us after Barbara and I had produced our first baby.

'Now your troubles will begin.'

'Sleepless nights . . . dirty nappies.'

'They're all right at this age, but just wait till they get older.'

'Just wait till they get to school. The problems are much easier when they're babies; at least you know where they are when they're in the pram.'

'One's easy to cope with. Just you wait till you've got two: then you'll know it.'

'Are you pleased?' (Which really meant: 'You didn't plan to have a baby just now did you?')

'Congratulations!'; 'Well done!' (There were some positive comments like this but not as many as the negative ones.)

Many of these comments came from other Christian parents.

I wonder what sort of view you have towards babies and children in general? Perhaps you have 'caught' some of this negativism from others. Maybe you grew up with it – your parents considered you a 'nuisance' factor. Do you hear yourself saying: 'I can't wait for you to go to school. You're driving me mad'; or, 'Just wait till *you* have to pay the phone bill'; or, 'If it wasn't for you we could have had a lovely holiday abroad this

year – children are so expensive to keep'; or, 'Go to your room
and stay there: you're nothing but a nuisance.'

In all sorts of ways we can say to babies and children, 'You're
in the way', 'You're spoiling my career', 'You're a pest', 'I wish
you belonged to someone else'. I recently found myself becoming
very defensive about this.

We were on holiday in Italy and our four children were having
a wonderful time in the hotel's swimming pool. They were
jumping, diving in, splashing each other, screaming and yelling
with excitement as they played.

Then I slowly became aware of the other people around the
pool. We were the only ones there with children. All the sun-
beds were filled with semi-naked adults trying to have a quiet
afternoon in the sun. They were all British, apart from two. One
by one they looked across to where mayhem was taking place.
They were definitely not amused.

At first I tried to ignore the glares and the muttered comments.
In the end I found myself constantly nagging the children, 'Stay
away from "that" side of the pool', and 'Keep the noise down',
and 'Jump in this side because you're annoying the grown-ups'.

It was ridiculous. The children were having the time of their
lives and enjoying a blissful playtime in the sun. However, the
adults present saw them simply as 'loud', 'uncontrolled', and a
'nuisance'. In fourteen years of parenthood I have never experienced such negative views towards children.

Thankfully not all British people are like the ones we met in
Italy on holiday. But this incident reminded me of how easy it is
for negative views to spoil the way we view children.

'Children are a gift from the LORD; they are a real blessing'
(Ps. 127:3 TEV). The adults at the pool-side in Italy would
certainly have had trouble with that verse. And I suspect all parents
find the words a challenge at some stage in their family life.

We're all tempted to see our children as an intrusion, a drain
on our resources, a distraction from the freedom to enjoy
ourselves. Yet if we're serious about letting Christ into our
homes, he can help us to see them differently. With his help we
discover that children are the best blessing we shall ever be given

in life, next to the gift of salvation itself. As we allow him to expose our weaknesses and challenge our attitudes, he can transform negative thinking into positive praise.

Recognising who is in control

Learning to see babies as a blessing begins by remembering how they are made. Medical science tells us that babies are the result of the human process of fertilisation. To 'make a baby', a man and a woman need to work together. It's worth considering just how this happens. It's a complicated process with a high rate of failure. Once a month (on average) a woman produces an egg inside her that travels down the Fallopian tubes and comes to rest in the womb. In order for fertilisation to take place the timing is crucial. The egg is only available for fertilisation for a few days. To achieve conception a man must ejaculate healthy sperm into the woman's vagina at this 'fertile' time of the month. Too early and the sperm will die before the egg can be reached; too late and the egg will no longer be fertile.

It is a very hit-and-miss affair. All sorts of things can go wrong. Even when the man's ejaculation does reach its target, the fertilised egg may fail to lodge in the lining of the womb. If it does manage to stay put, the next nine months can bring all sorts of threats to the well-being of the developing foetus.

As for the process of delivery itself, this can be the most dangerous moment in any of our lives, not least for the woman giving birth. I have been present at the birth of all our children, and each time I've been amazed at how Barbara has managed to survive the experience. Thank God he made me a man: it was bad enough just being a helpless onlooker!

After medical science has said all it wants to say, the Bible tells us more. Conception is a lot more than two people getting their act together. For instance, God told Jeremiah: 'Before I formed you in the womb I knew you' (Jer. 1:5). This tells us two important details about the process of conception and birth.

1 Life is no accident

Jeremiah had a difficult job to do. He had been called by God to say things that most people didn't want to hear. There would be many times in his life when he would be tempted to give up his ministry. But the words God spoke to him reminded him that he was not alive in Israel at that time in history by chance. His life had purpose and meaning. Indeed God was telling him that his life was planned even before his parents had anything to do with it.

This wasn't a new truth. God had said as much to Abraham: 'I will bless Sarah and will surely give you a son by her' (Gen. 17:16). No wonder Abraham laughed. If he had been around today, he would have been due for a telegram from the Queen on his next birthday. Meanwhile Sarah had long since proved that babies were not her speciality.

The words of the psalmist echoed this truth too: 'The days allotted to me had all been recorded in your book, before any of them ever began' (Ps. 139:16 TEV). The Bible reminds us again and again that life comes from God. As human beings we share in his work of creation, but we do not control when or how it takes place.

If we can begin to see that all our children come to us through God's creative activity in us then we shall look at them differently. Barbara and I have been challenged three times about this as parents.

Only one of our children was conceived by deliberate choice, though we have used a reliable method of contraception all our married life. The rest have just come along on the way. It has therefore been important for us to see each of them as a gift from God.

This has been particularly important when our family life has been hard. At one point we had four children under five. It was no joke. I dreaded meal times when the babies had to be fed. It was a 'scream – feed', 'cry – carry', 'moan – rock' sort of life-style.

When we moved to Bromley with three children we made up

our minds that if we wanted any more children we would
definitely have to wait. Our house was a small three-bedroomed
end-of-terrace. In practice it was really only two-bedroomed,
because I needed one of the rooms upstairs for my study.
Therefore, when Elizabeth came along we had to take a deep
breath and squeeze in. Her conception seemed like very bad
planning at the time. People had stopped saying things like,
'Now your troubles will begin'; they said instead, 'How will you
cope?'! Somehow, by the grace of God, we did and each of the
children has been a great blessing to us in different ways.

2   Life is sacred

The National Health Service has not always lived up to our
expectations. We once had to put up with a very rude paediatri-
cian as our consultant. Some of the ante-natal care we've been
through has been very oppressive and problem orientated. There
have been times when it has seemed that life is only a matter of
science, medicine and enormous risk. I didn't appreciate how
painful this could be until Barbara had a miscarriage in June
1990.

When it happened we were both devastated. The grisly process
of a D & C (dilation and curettage – a minor operation to scrape
the lining of the womb) didn't help; but I found the careless
attitude of medical people was the last straw. 'You can always try
for another', was the stock answer we were given. 'You've got
four; that's something to be grateful about,' was another. However, the description of our lost baby as 'the products of
conception' defied belief. This was a human being that people
were talking about – our son or daughter.

I found the whole incident very chilling indeed. It is only now,
some years later, that I find myself beginning to come to terms
with what happened. The tragedy was made worse when the
same thing happened in September of that year. No counselling
was given or suggested. Some people were sympathetic, but on
the whole it was dismissed as being 'one of those things'. Two
children, dismissed as if they never existed.

The Bible reminds us that the contents of the womb and what goes on inside there are sacred:

'For you created my inmost being; you knit me together in my mother's womb . . . When I was woven together in the depths of the earth, your eyes saw my unformed body' (Ps. 139:13–16).

These words remind us that life does not begin at birth; it begins the moment God's activity takes place to form a new human being; this activity is *sacred*.

Seeing all life as sacred will help us to develop the right attitudes to babies. The abortion law of 1967 has done more to destroy the sanctity of the womb than any other act in human history. Whatever the arguments about the alternative 'back-street' abortions and 'Frankenstein-type devices', it is impossible to justify the invasion of this sacred space with a blunt instrument of destruction. The 'products of conception' belong to God's hand and not the incinerator of a hospital.

There is a reason why our children are created and there is also a reason why sometimes this goes wrong. It is no accident. Babies cannot be born by accident; they can only be brought into existence through the amazing power of a creator God who made the first human being from something so apparently ordinary as a bit of dust.

When you and I look at our children we need constantly to remind ourselves: this person is a gift from God. They're not here by accident. They're here for a purpose, and that main purpose is the blessing of our marriage, home and world. God told Abram, 'all peoples on earth will be blessed through you' (Gen. 12:3): those of us who count ourselves as being God's children are, if we can comprehend it, the result of that blessing. Can we not learn to see our children like this too? Through our children God desires to bless the earth. We'll look at this again in the final chapter.

Adjusting to a new life

When we become parents for the first time and welcome a new human life into our home, it takes time to get used to the idea. I didn't appreciate this at all when we had our first baby. Like many other parents-to-be, Barbara and I went along to 'Parent-craft classes' designed to prepare us for junior's arrival. I don't remember much about the classes, though I think they were generally good. However, I do remember a film we watched.

It was a documentary, describing a couple's reaction to the birth of their first child. One of the parents said, 'It took me six months to get used to the idea of the baby. Until then it was "just there". It didn't seem real before that.'

After hearing that I muttered to Barbara, 'Well that's a load of nonsense. How can it take so long to adjust to having a baby in the house?' I was sure the film was wrong. All my life I'd had children around me. When I was at home I helped look after three babies. I was used to babies. What could be simpler than having one of my own?

But I was wrong. When it came to the birth of our eldest son the film proved to be right. When I held Nathaniel in my arms on 26 August 1980 he seemed real enough. When we took him home to our flat in Gillingham he soon made his presence felt: his clutter (and crying) seemed to be everywhere. But it was at least six months before I felt that he belonged to us and that he was really ours. I cannot really explain this. Perhaps your experience is quite different.

We should not take the adjustment to babies for granted. When a new person is added to our home everything is different. It is not surprising that when they come into our lives, things are never quite the same. The same is true when a person is taken from our home through death or some other form of separation. Parenthood is a process of getting used to constant changes in our home.

This isn't easy. One of the frequent mistakes I make is to think I should succeed at this parenthood business first time. 'After all,' I say to myself, 'I had marvellous opportunities when I was growing up to learn about babies. I've trained as a teacher and know all about child psychology and human development. Since becoming a vicar I have constantly found myself in contact with children. All this must count for something.'

But putting Christ at the centre of our parenting means recognising when and where we fail. It may sound great to have 2.4 children who are well-adjusted, don't pick their nose in public, have no unsociable habits, always do well at school, appear in every school production and who convince the teachers they are 'great kids' and the church folk they are 'terrific kids'. Real life is a little different. No amount of training or experience can prepare us for some of the adjustments that come with becoming a parent.

Sex during pregnancy

How many of us are prepared for the disruption that children cause in our sex lives? Just as we men get used to having it 3.8 times a week the women start feeling sick. It's nothing personal, but the idea of you putting your tongue in her mouth – let alone your penis somewhere even more intimate – is a big 'no-no'.

Eventually (if you're fortunate), the sickness settles down and things start to get back to normal again. You climb into bed and whisper sweet nothings in her ear. Then, just as you are about to make a passionate advance, you find she has slipped into a pre-natal coma. Your urgent question: 'Are you asleep?' receives no response.

Then of course there's this bump which is beginning to come between you. All the books tell you there's a way round it, but when you try this out it doesn't seem to work as they say it should. As the big day approaches, the risk of premature labour proves to be a particularly effective passion-killer and so it's just a kiss and a cuddle for now.

Eventually the person who has been slowly growing in between you at last moves out into the big wide world. The sight of all that blood and the distress that goes with it is enough to put even me off sex for a few weeks. But as the remains of the bump go, and the blood stops flowing, the day for human passions to be released approaches. Alleluia!

You snuggle into bed covered in aftershave and ready to make up for lost time. Taking your beloved in your arms, you give her a long lingering kiss. And then it happens: you hear a noise. No it's not a gurgle or a contented sigh, it's you-know-who making sure that your sex life will never be the same again!

A good night's sleep?

When Barbara and I first got married we used to go to bed (to sleep!) at 10 p.m. and not wake up until gone 7 a.m. the next day. As children came into our home, all that began to change. When Nathaniel was born we only had one bedroom, so he had to sleep in the cot next to our bed. For weeks (it seemed like years) he would wake up just as we snuggled down into bed. It was as though the contented sound of his parents dozing off was the signal to let loose with his lungs.

Then there was the drinks routine with Elizabeth. She is our youngest, and was a very different sort of baby from her three brothers. They all settled down to sleeping through the night by six months. Not so little Lizzy. She continued to wake up every night for a feed long past the half-year mark. Eventually a drink of blackcurrant replaced the milk she was given. But at eighteen months she still woke up every night.

When your first three have behaved quite differently you begin to wonder why the fourth is being so difficult. What had we done wrong? How could we get her out of this bad habit? Should we just leave her to cry? Would she ever grow out of this wearing routine?

The breakthrough came one winter's night. It was cold, I was tired and Elizabeth was old enough to get out of bed herself. Stumbling in a stupor to the landing, I met my beautiful but exhausting daughter as she pattered out of her room. 'Elizabeth, this has got to stop!' I said, imagining that this two-year-old understood perfectly well what I was going on about. 'What is it you want?' I added.

'Want a drink ...' she replied rather sheepishly, wondering why this grown-up was being so grumpy and wishing that the other one (who wasn't half so grouchy in the middle of the night) was on the landing instead.

'Well here's your drink,' I said, putting it on the landing outside her bedroom door. 'If you want a drink then help yourself and then go back to bed. Understood?'

'Yes Daddy,' she said, in between slurps from her cup of juice. And then, picking her up and giving her a big hug, I put her back to bed.

The lecture on the landing at 3 a.m. worked. I was amazed. Elizabeth never woke up crying for a drink again. She continued waking up, but always came out on to the landing and helped herself instead. Was she cured? Well, yes – sort of. The only trouble was that after satisfying her thirst she came into our bedroom and asked Mummy to come to put her back to bed again!

Adjusting to babies takes time. It takes a lifetime, so we need to be patient with ourselves when we find that the going gets really hard. Other parents have been there before us, and more importantly Jesus has gone ahead of us. He knows what all our tomorrows are going to bring. Nothing escapes his attention – not even a parent's desire to have sex and a good night's sleep.

God's promise to our children

Part of this process of adjustment to a new person in our home is the need to revise our expectations of them. As our children develop and change, so we need to develop and change the way we look at them. But there is one attitude which should stay constant throughout our lives: it is the conviction that God is always at work in our children. The Bible teaches quite clearly that God's covenant love for us extends to our children as well. His promise of blessing to Abraham was a promise to his children and their descendants:

Then God said to Abraham, 'As for you, you must keep my covenant, you and your descendants after you for the generations to come. This is my covenant with you and your descendants after you, the covenant you are to keep: Every male among you shall be circumcised. You are to undergo circumcision, and it will be the sign of the covenant between me and you. For the generations to come every male among you who is eight days old must be circumcised, including those born in your household or bought with money from a foreigner – those who are not your offspring. Whether born in your household or bought with your money, they must be circumcised. My covenant in your flesh is to be an everlasting covenant. Any uncircumcised male, who has not been circumcised in the flesh, will be cut off from his people; he has broken my covenant' (Gen. 17:9–14).

It is absurd to let Christ into our sex lives, as we thought about in chapter 3, and then keep him out of our children's lives. The act of circumcision is the most graphic visual aid possible to make this point. To put it bluntly, every time a Jewish husband put his erect penis into his wife's vagina, the scar on his penis was a powerful reminder from God: the seed he was about to ejaculate was the on-going promise of blessing that began with Abraham.

All males were automatically initiated into this covenant. They were not 'left to make up their own minds' when they were older. They were in the covenant from the very beginning. The circumcision of a man's penis remained a physical and spiritual signpost to the fact that God's people belong to him – parents, children, grandchildren, great-grandchildren, and even those who share our home with us (Gen. 17:12–13).

Of course it was possible for them to rebel against God, and the Old Testament tracks the record of Israel's frequent breaking of the covenant. Although God desires that everyone should come to a knowledge of the truth and experience salvation (Ezek. 18:23–32), Jesus knew that the power of sin was such that most people preferred the easy way to 'the narrow way' (Matt. 7:13–14). He also warned the religious leaders of his day that being children of Abraham entailed more than just an inherited

scar on their anatomy; the real test was whether they reflected
the family likeness (see John 8:31–59).

God's covenant with his people today is a new covenant based
upon the person and work of Christ. It is a covenant that is far
superior to the old one (see Heb. 8:1–13). The sign of this
covenant has changed. The act of circumcision has been replaced
by the sacrament of baptism. But the covenant is still based on
the same principle of God's amazing, unconditional, undeserved
love.

As Christian parents we need not be afraid to have our babies
baptised and initiated into a covenant that is for us, for them and
for their children's children. When they grow up and are old
enough to understand what this means, they will have the chance
to opt out of this if that is (unhappily) what they choose to do.
But for their long-term good and benefit, we should treat them
as Christians until they decide to choose otherwise.

Part of this understanding of covenant love means expecting
great things from our children. The Bible teaches us that all
human beings are made in the image of God (Gen. 1:27). This
includes those who reject God as well as those who love and
follow him. However, those who are brought within the covenant
of God's love have been given a unique opportunity in human
history.

Our homes and families can be used by God to bring the
knowledge of his love and salvation to the community we live in.
Our children are a vital part of this. We have found this very
humbling as we've watched how God can use us in his plan for
the salvation of his world.

When we moved to a parish in the Lake District there were
very few children in church on a Sunday. Our four became an
'instant Sunday school class' and they attracted more. They
didn't go round to their friends 'preaching the gospel'. Elizabeth
and Elliott were pre-school when we first moved in and could
hardly be expected to give their testimony!

However their very presence in the church had a profound
impact: other children started coming to church who had never
come before. Their presence in our home proved to be one of

the greatest blessings we ever shared during our ministry as a family there; without them we could never have accomplished the things we did. The lasting children's work that continues in that parish today, long after we have departed, is due to the Spirit of God using our home and children to reach others with the wonderful news of God's love.

Let's expect God to be at work in our children and through our children: they are given to us to be a blessing. The baby in a pram is a great starter for conversations with other mums. The toddler at playgroup is a marvellous introduction to other parents who have struggles like us but don't yet know that Christ's power can help their home. The child starting school opens up for us all sorts of doors into relationships with people in our community whom we wouldn't otherwise meet.

In this decade of evangelism God wants to use all the resources he has given us to show his love to the world. Our homes and families are the most precious and powerful resource we will ever be given. Have great expectations of your children, because God has.

Realistic goals

As well as having great expectations for our children we need to be sensible. Children are not expendable. Our ambitions for them need to be realistic. Let me illustrate.

From time to time we play football together as a family. This works quite well, when Dad (who hates football) is prepared to co-operate. We have two teams of three.

Elizabeth likes playing in goal, so when she plays we make the goal size a reasonable width. If it is too wide, she has no hope of being able to save any goals. If it is too small, her older brothers whinge continually that 'it's not fair'. We need to get the goal just right.

The same applies when it comes to our expectations of our children. I find myself frequently failing in this area of family life, because I forget that my children are children. I constantly need reminding that they are not adults in smaller bodies; they

are new people who need time and freedom to develop into the
people God wants them to be.

If I could change one of the mistakes I have made over the last
fourteen years it would be this: I would be more realistic about
what I expect from my children and not compel them to be like
me – that isn't why God made them. He made them to be like
Christ.

Part of this realism about our children must also be a sensible
doctrine of sin. Children are not born perfect. King David
recognised this. After his adultery with Bathsheba (2 Sam. 11)
and the terrible consequences which followed, David became
acutely aware of how far back the roots of his sin went:

> Wash away all my iniquity and cleanse me from my sin. For I
> know my transgressions, and my sin is always before me.
> Against you you only, have I sinned and done what is evil in
> your sight, so that you are proved right when you speak and
> justified when you judge. Surely I have been a sinner from
> birth, sinful from the time my mother conceived me
> (Ps. 51:2–5).

Children are born with sinful natures. The first parents recognised this. If it wasn't for the intervention of our almighty and
loving God, the opening chapters of the Bible would make
depressing reading.

Adam and Eve's first child Cain was a murderer. Cain's great-
great-great-grandson was so insecure that he promised to visit
terrible consequences on anyone who crossed him (Gen. 4:23–4);
by the time we get to chapter 5 God decided it was time to draw
a line under the human race and start again.

Our families are not immune from the poison of sin, and we
need to recognise it when we see it in our children. When God
told Eve, 'I will greatly increase your pains in childbearing; with
pain you will give birth to children' (Gen. 3:16) it was more than
just physical pain that he had in mind. Surely the greatest pain
for the first parents was the sorrow at seeing their eldest son
becoming trapped and mastered by sin.

The same can happen in our homes. Christ is the only one who has the power to do something about this and as we bring his love and power into our children's lives, he will. We'll be taking a closer look at how some of this might work out in practice in the next two chapters. For the moment, let me summarise what I have been trying to say like this.

It was February 1980. Hyde Park was cold and deserted except for the remainder of autumn leaves and the occasional jogger. The winter sun was setting over Kensington Palace, creating a rather tired golden haze. Two figures crossed the park from west to east, along one of the many paths that wind through this oasis of nature in the heart of the big city. They were arm in arm, snuggled up together against the chilling frosty air.

They were pushing a smart blue pram with shiny chrome-silver wheels. There was no baby inside – only a suitcase and other belongings which the couple had brought with them after getting off the train at Paddington Station.

The smiles from the passing joggers had nothing to do with the contents of the pram, nor with the unusual sight of a pram in Hyde Park at that time of year. They were smiling at the large red and white 'L' plate affixed to the front.

The couple didn't mind the funny looks and comments as they steered their way past Buckingham Palace on to Victoria Station. They were happy. In less than five months they would be the proud parents of Nathaniel Robert Ireton.

Barbara and I kept the 'L' plate which friends had given us when we bought that pram. It's been in our family for many years, though I have replaced it with a new magnetic one now.

The pram has long since been stored away. But the 'L' plate is fixed on to the metal filing cabinet in my study, which I pass every time I leave the room. I've kept it there as a constant reminder that in this game of family life, I am still a learner.

All those years ago our pram rode empty across London. We had no idea who would fill it or how many children God would be pleased to send us as we've travelled along through life. There have been moments when the travelling has been hard going and the destination very difficult to find, and moments too when I've felt like turning back. But always as we have sought Christ's way forward, he has seen us through.

As our babies have grown into children and children turned into teenagers, we have travelled back as a family each year to that timeless human home and family where God himself chose to come and live in person. In the unpromising and temporary home of a stable, in the untried and inexperienced love of two new parents, and in the inescapable chill of a moral, economic and political winter we find a God of power entering in. If God loved the world so much that he did this, then we can have complete confidence that whatever happens to our family life, he will not desert us when we need his help.

But now, this is what the LORD says – he who created you, O Jacob, he who formed you, O Israel: 'Fear not, for I have redeemed you; I have called you by name; you are mine. When you pass through the waters, I will be with you; and when you pass through the rivers, they will not sweep over you. When you walk through the fire, you will not be burned; the flames will not set you ablaze. For I am the LORD, your God, the Holy One of Israel, your Saviour' (Isa. 43:1–3).

6

CHAOS

Chaos can invade family life in any number of ways. Let me describe three chaotic scenes from our experience. Maybe you will identify with one or more of them.

Scene 1   Harvest chaos

It was a pleasant October day. Autumn had settled on the Lake District. The leaves were changing rapidly from soft relaxing shades of green, to striking, vivid splashes of red, orange and brown along the borders of the open fields. The fells, weathered and smoothed by countless years of wind and rain, reflected the autumn gold of a harvest sunset. What could interrupt such order, such exquisite beauty, such captivating scenery that seemed almost to enfold you in its outstretched arms?

Head-lice! Yes, those grotty little creatures that hide behind the ears and in the nape of the neck, sucking your blood and multiplying – literally – like fleas. Yuck. The very mention of them makes my head start to itch.

Nitty Nora the head explorer – otherwise known as the school nurse – had discovered 'the plague' in our children's hair on Friday. It was harvest weekend at Matterdale Church, our first harvest there since moving from London. That night was harvest supper-time, and all our children had to be treated for head-lice.

The trouble was, we didn't discover it until they came home from school with a note. We had no lotion to treat them with, the doctor's surgery was a twenty-mile round trip away, and we were all expected to be at Matterdale for this annual harvest event.

Things were made worse by the method of treatment that these nasty little chaos-creators require. Head-lice are so persistent that each year they have to be treated with different chemicals. If they receive the same treatment year after year they become resistant to it and immune to its effects.

This year it was the turn of Prioderm. Let me describe to you what this revolting stuff is like.

It isn't a shampoo, like Lyclear or other similar treatments. It's an oil-type substance. You need a mask when applying it to children's hair because the fumes that it gives off make you retch. The worst is yet to come. In order for this treatment to be fully effective and to kill all the eggs, it needs to be left on the hair for at least two hours – and preferably overnight. While it's doing its job, it makes your head look like it's been recently dipped in left over chip-fat.

This invasion of chaos left us with three options:

Option one Leave the head-lice untreated and risk spreading them to the other children at the supper. This course of action was definitely out. Rumour had it that there was an epidemic of head-lice in the Penrith area that year. We knew what it was like to have to treat four children with Prioderm; we didn't wish this horror on anyone else.

Option two Abandon the idea of all of us going to the harvest supper, which meant leaving the children at home with Barbara while I went on alone. This would certainly solve the problem of having to get the treatment done before 7 p.m. I could collect the prescription from the surgery in Penrith, leaving Barbara to do the awful bit, and enjoy a pleasant supper without having to keep my eyes on all the children while trying to make polite conversation with the locals. But this option had two major drawbacks.

This was our first harvest event at Matterdale. It would look rather odd if I turned up for it without any of the family with me, especially as the event had been billed as a 'meet the new vicar and his family' occasion. How would I explain the children's absence to these people whom I hardly knew? . . . 'I'm sorry, Barbara and the children couldn't make it tonight. They've got head-lice.'

What a wonderful start to making relationships with complete strangers that would be. I could just imagine the 'crack'[1] around the village the next day:

'Did you meet the new vicar last night?'

'Yes. Seems a nice enough chap. Very young. Didn't get to meet his wife and children though. They'd all got head-lice.'

'Oh . . .'

Option three Treat everyone before the deadline of 7 p.m. In the end, we opted for this third, most chaotic way of tackling the chaos. I don't know how we did it, looking back. Treating four children aged two to seven, getting them something to eat (the Harvest Supper was not a full meal), trying to sort out all the objections to this 'awful stuff on my hair' and look like a typical vicarage family (whatever that is) by 7 p.m. was a nightmare. But we turned up, only a few minutes late. If people had only seen us in the chaos beforehand, they might have had rather different views about how well-organised we seemed to be as a family. Head-lice have become an almost annual event in our home, and each time they invade they bring chaos with them.

Scene 2   Hospital chaos

In early November 1990 we moved from a stunning view of Helvellyn across Cumbrian mountains, to a monochrome housing estate with uninterrupted views of double glazing land (not my description; a previous resident described Falconwood in these rather cruel terms). It was a bit of a shock to the system. My previous parish was 120 square miles with 1,800 residents. Falconwood is about 1.2 square miles with about 7,000 people.

A few weeks after moving in, Elliott was admitted to hospital. He had been complaining of pains in his legs for some time. To begin with we just kept a close eye on him; we assumed he was experiencing some sort of 'growing pains'. His intense dislike of his new school in London, and his desire to have time off from it made us suspect that this might not be just a physiological problem.

He had very good reason to want to stay away from school; he was beaten up on his first day there. What an introduction. This had been a horrible experience for him; he was barely seven years old.

When he began having trouble walking, we realised that there must be something more seriously wrong with him. After taking him to our local GP we ended up in casualty, waiting to see a consultant. This was to be the beginning of a long dark tunnel of chaos.

The doctor who examined him admitted him to hospital for observation and put his left leg in traction. Barbara and I felt sick inside. This was our first weekend at the new church and here we were with a child in hospital, family hundreds of miles away, friends in the parish as yet non-existent and three other children to care for. They were finding it hard enough adjusting to their new environment without being separated from their brother and mum, who stayed in hospital with him.

I am not good at family separations, as you will find out in a later chapter on that subject. When Barbara was in hospital after giving birth to Nathaniel, I used to count the hours until visiting time. I hated every moment of being apart on that occasion.

The experience with Elliott was far worse. No one seemed to know what was the matter with him. They gave him a series of tests and told us that he might have Perthes' disease.

This is a rare but potentially serious bone problem. It begins with the child limping and complaining of pain in the knee and it usually affects the thigh bone. Because this disease is usually progressive and has three stages it can't be diagnosed right away. While the doctors guessed and we prayed, Elliott spent a week on his back with weights dangling from his leg, feeling very sorry for himself.

His stay in hospital was not helped by the fact that the

children's ward was badly staffed. The nurses left Barbara to wash him and make sure he was properly fed. They rarely offered any help, and the general standard of care he was given was disgraceful. Given different circumstances I would have considered suing the hospital for negligence. At the time, my only concern was to help Elliott get better and not do anything which might prejudice his treatment.

With Christmas just a few days away, we somehow managed to survive. Elliott was eventually discharged from hospital on a 'wait and see' basis. Meanwhile, we tried to pick up the pieces of our family life. This unwelcome chaos left Barbara and me physically and emotionally shattered and wondering where God was in all of this.

Scene 3   Ultimate chaos

Horrible experiences in family life often seem different when we look back on them. They usually take on a less grotesque appearance than when we're stuck in the middle of them. We can even forget them in time! But one scene of family chaos will live with me for a long time.

It was May 1982. Barbara and I had just returned from a restful and refreshing break in Cheltenham. We'd been staying with Nathaniel's godparents, who have been good friends to us since student teacher days. The weather had been perfect. The break had helped to restore both of us after an exhausting few months. All seemed well with the world. But this was soon to change.

Our home in those days was a three-bedroomed, end-of-terrace with a good sized garden. It was just a short walk from Oak Hill College in north London. I was nearing the end of my first year of training for the Anglican ministry. We had two children, Nathaniel aged twenty-one months, and Samuel just eight weeks old.

Barbara had had a difficult pregnancy with Samuel, and had spent some weeks in hospital. This meant I was at home with Nathaniel full time and had fallen very much behind with my college work. Even so, the week's holiday had revitalised us both, and I drove home eager to get started on the pile of assignments waiting for me. However, the moment we opened the front door we smelt trouble – literally.

The freezer in the hallway had broken down while we were away, and the smell of rotting food hit us as soon as we came in. Unfortunately, our house contents insurance didn't cover this particular risk, so all the food was lost. This was a real financial set-back for us because we had no regular income. The grant which I received from church authorities paid for college tuition and just about covered the rent, but we had to trust the Lord to provide for all our other living expenses.

Just as all this began to sink in, Samuel started screaming. There was nothing wrong with him; he just cried and cried and cried for the next twenty-four hours. We picked him up, we patted his back, we paced the floor with him, we rocked him in the pram. We tried everything, but he just screamed.

Fortunately, our eldest son Nathaniel didn't follow suit, but even he seemed out of sorts for some reason. Family life seemed to be getting completely out of hand. By Monday morning, I was convinced things couldn't get any worse. Until, that is, I took the car in for its MOT. The verdict from the garage was the final straw. To repair the car and make it roadworthy again would cost over three hundred pounds: this was three hundred times more than the resources we had available to meet the bill. I couldn't believe it.

Your experiences of chaos in family life may be different from mine. But when chaos invades our lives, how can Chist help us to make sense of it? Here are three tips for coping with chaos when it comes.

1 Accept it

There isn't much you can do to avoid chaos in the home. When it comes it seems to take on a life of its own while you stand by helplessly.

Our children's bedrooms are a good example of this. One

summer we decided to bring order to our son's room. His walls were a mess, his furniture rather tatty and the room seemed generally 'messy'. So we painted the ceiling, papered the walls, coloured the furniture and woodwork in matching signal red, then moved the owner back in. The result was rather surprising.

The room was a great improvement; it looked bright and clean and welcoming, but a few weeks later it seemed to be back to its 'messy' feel again. It's hard to say why; it just felt messy, even when it was reasonably tidy.

We didn't fully understand why this was until some time later. By this stage Elizabeth, who had been sharing a room with one of her brothers, was getting to the age where she needed a room of her own. So between them they agreed to a swap. Two of the boys moved into the biggest room and Elizabeth took over the recently decorated room. A few weeks later I was walking past Elizabeth's 'new' bedroom when I suddenly realised it looked different. It still had toys, books, clothes and all the usual things in it. But it was immaculately tidy and neat. The whole room had a completely different feel about it. Meanwhile, the chaos hadn't left the house: it had moved to the other end of the hallway where 'Mr Messy' had moved in with one of his brothers!

This incident has taught me something important about chaos. However much you and I try to control it and make it stop, chaos has a life of its own. If you shift it from one place, you find it popping up somewhere else. Chaos cannot be avoided in family life. Just when you think you've got it cornered in one place, it suddenly breaks out somewhere else.

The incident with the bedrooms doesn't tell the whole story. Elizabeth may have brought order into the chaos her brother left behind, but when she is doing her hair in the morning a rather different form of chaos has been known to break out!

Learning to accept chaos as an inevitable part of family life can help to prevent us from getting too depressed by it. Every Christmas we celebrate a historic event that was shrouded in its own form of chaos. The cards may beautify the stable, but there's no getting away from the chaos.

Think of it for a moment. Mary and Joseph travelling the

eighty- or ninety-mile journey from Nazareth in the north to Bethlehem in the south. This was a hard enough trip at the best of time. But, being nine months pregnant, Mary must have suffered badly. When they arrived at their destination they must have wondered, like we do sometimes, whether they would survive the chaos that was invading their lives.

As Joseph was turned away from the one place that could give his family a comfortable start in life, he must have wondered whether things could get much worse. The decision to have a baby just now hadn't been his; the choice of the uncomfortable and difficult journey to Bethlehem hadn't been his; even the end result of Mary's labour wasn't his. We need look no further than the stable in Bethlehem for the evidence that even the most important human family in history was not immune from this experience called chaos.

Take courage if the road your family life is on at the moment seems to be through the tunnel of chaos: a lot of other families have been through this dark place too and eventually emerged safely from the other side.

2   Remember who's in control of it

Chaos doesn't take God by surprise. We may be surprised by it. We may not be prepared for it. But this is never true of God. As we look at the way Jesus handled chaos when he was a grown man, we can see the absolute authority and power he has over everything that happens. We could go to many stories in the Gospels to illustrate this. Let's look at just one. It comes in Matthew 8, Mark 4, and Luke 8.

Jesus was out on Lake Galilee with his disciples. There was nothing unusual about this. As time went by, his teaching and power to heal became famous. He couldn't go anywhere without attracting a crowd. The lake became a safe place for him to escape from people's demands for a few hours.

On this occasion, he was so exhausted from his work that he fell asleep in the back of the boat shortly after they left the shore. He must have been in a very deep sleep because the gathering

storm didn't even cause him to stir. The boat began rocking
violently, tossed back and forth by the waves.

Galilee was notorious for sudden storms. It could be calm and
still one minute; in the next, you could find yourself in the
middle of a hurricane. The disciples on board that night weren't
all fishermen, but even those who were began to worry about
this violent squall. There had been stories of ships lost at sea
with no survivors. Rumour had it that evil spirits inhabited the
waters and only Roman gods could keep you safe when the sea
got out of hand. The disciples didn't believe this; most Jews
wouldn't. But the chaotic weather that had come upon them
seemed more sinister than wild. It seemed to have something
personal against them. Every attempt they made to get the ship
under control again was ripped from their hands by the terrible
winds.

As the storm grew worse, the disciples' minds were invaded by
nagging doubts. Jesus had cured sick people. He'd got rid of
demons. He preached better than anyone in the world. But,
could he do anything about an out-of-control storm?

Surely, they thought, he would wake up in a minute. Surely
the splashing water that was lapping around his feet would bring
him to life and he would help them. Surely he couldn't sleep
through all this? Surely anyone in their right mind would wake
up when disaster threatened all their lives, including his own.

And so in a terrible panic, they went over to wake him, shaking
him – almost violently – and bellowing at him above the terrible
noise of the wind.

'Don't you care if we're all going to drown?' some said.

'Lord, save us! We're going to drown,' others added.

It was an embarrassing moment: twelve grown men, some of
them experienced fishermen who well knew the terrible weather
on Lake Galilee, crying out in blind fear to a teacher who'd
never caught a fish in his life.

For those few moments on board the creaking fishing boat,
chaos seemed to reign. It ruled over the weather. It ruled over
the hearts of the disciples, and looked as if it was about to
swallow them all up in a huge overwhelming gulp. Somehow,

amid the seething storm, Jesus managed to stand up – which was more than the disciples could do. He seemed completely in control; not even the slightest sign of fear on his face. And when he spoke his voice reminded you of Psalm 29:

> The voice of the LORD is over the waters; the God of glory thunders, the LORD thunders over the mighty waters. The voice of the LORD is powerful (vv. 3–4).

At that instant, the storm came to an abrupt end. It was uncanny, almost eerie. Sometimes a storm would suddenly begin to ease off, but the waves would always take a bit longer to settle down.

The disciples had never seen anything in their lives like this before. It was as though the weather knew the person standing up in the boat, and didn't dare to disobey his voice even for a split second. The moment he told the wind to 'shut up', it stopped howling. The second he commanded the waves to 'sit down' they settled down into a spirit-level calm.

It was not the chaos that the disciples found themselves in awe of; it was the person standing up in the boat. He knew all about the chaos that was raging all around them and showed his power to control the uncontrollable. No wonder they were terrified of Jesus that night. There was something about the way he spoke which made them tremble inside. It felt as if Almighty God was in the boat.

Whenever chaos descends upon us and we feel caught in a family-life storm, we need to remember who is in charge of our lives. Troubles will try to throw us about and we may get badly shaken by them, but with Christ in our homes we do not need to be afraid of drowning. Psalm 93 says:

> The seas have lifted up, O LORD, the seas have lifted up their voice; the seas have lifted up their pounding waves. [But] Mightier than the thunder of the great waters, mightier than the breakers of the sea – the LORD on high is mighty (vv. 3–4).

Our God reigns

Before we move on, let me take you back to May 1982 and share a personal example of God reigning over our chaos. The chaos in our food supply when our freezer broke down could not be suddenly taken away. We had to throw everything in the dustbin. The chaos in our transport arrangements when our ancient car failed its MOT had to be faced. We would have liked to have managed without a car, but this just wasn't practical. The chaos in my academic work caused by three months of disruption to our home life could not be easily overcome. I had less than a month to write fifteen weeks' worth of work.

Yet God showed me that he was fully in charge of all this chaos. The day my car came back from its failed MOT, a friend from college called and managed to get it repaired for less than half the original quote. That same week a cheque for a thousand pounds arrived in the post quite unexpectedly, and by the end of term the eleven assignments I had to write were all finished and (with one exception) received straight 'A's.

Coincidence? Just 'good luck'? A fluke? No. This was chaos-control by an almighty God who is faithful beyond our wildest seas. Christ never promised us a life free from chaos, but he did promise he would always be with us – even if at times it seems as though he's in the back of the boat fast asleep.

3   Find a safe place to hide

When we visited Italy in 1994, we took the children to see the city of Pompeii. Acres of ruins are all that's left of a once great civilisation. You can see the houses where people used to live and stand in gardens and courtyards of those who had been wealthy citizens. In the quiet music of a dancing fountain, you can hear the echo of a culture that used to control the known world.

In AD 79 the entire population of Pompeii was destroyed when Mount Vesuvius blew itself apart. The people were not killed by red-hot lava flow, but by the gas and ash that rained down upon the area for days, as the terrible effects of a volcanic eruption took their toll. No one survived that particular chaos.

In the remains of the city, archaeologists found empty pockets in the volcanic ash which, when filled with plaster, turned out to be the remains of human beings. They had been frozen in time at the exact moment that the eruption took place. It is a pitiful sight. There is man, crouching to hide his face from the fumes and a group of people lying down together in a 'refuge' where they thought they could escape. In Herculaneum a few miles away, an up-turned boat has just been discovered and underneath it the remains of others who tried to hide. In the museum you see the famous 'petrified' dog lying on its back with its feet in the air.

The only people who did survive this disaster were those who ran away before the eruption took place. There were several 'warnings' before the catastrophe. Among the ruins there is evidence that after the great earthquake of AD 62, some people abandoned their properties and therefore escaped the final destruction fifteen years later.

The Christian faith offers families a safe hiding-place when we're up against it. Some of the chaos which we face is entirely predictable. There's the 'terrible twos'; the 'temper tantrums'; the adolescent rebellion; the morning after the party before. Bringing Christ into our homes gives us a safe place to hide when we find the chaos overwhelming us. And, when a way of escape cannot be found, he is able to help us endure.

For some of this will mean admitting defeat. We may need to accept the fact that we cannot cope with the toddler's tantrums, or the teenager's waywardness. Barbara is much better with eleven-to-thirteen-year-olds than I am. For some reason I find that this age group really winds me up! I've learnt to cope with this shortcoming over the years and have worked hard to relate to this pre-teenage group. But I am a failure compared to my wife.

In practice this means being prepared to let Barbara take over when I can't cope. This may sound like escapism, but in fact it is applying 1 Corinthians 12 to our parenting. One parent will have a gift in one area of family life, another will be gifted in a different area. God has made us to work together in our families and make use of the resources he has richly provided.

I like to think I'm good with children of any age but I know in my heart this is not true. Facing up to it makes the chaos much more understandable. Therefore I can endure it a little better.

Christ himself offers a unique place to run to and hide when the chaos gets too great. There will be times in all our families when none of the theories work and all our available resources are exhausted. Our family life has become like a prison – someone has locked us in and thrown away the key.

Martin and Pat felt like this. Pat had grown up in a large family in the inner city and always wanted to have children of her own. When she got married it turned out that she was infertile, so she and Martin adopted a child instead. By the grace of God, a few years later Pat became pregnant.

The birth defied medical science; the parents were overjoyed. Unfortunately, when Pat came home from hospital, she began to suffer from severe post-natal depression. It lasted for many years.

I spoke to her, prayed with her and tried to encourage her over a long period of time. But depression is a terrible chaos for a family to live with.

Martin was amazing. He remained so loyal and faithful to his wife. He stood by her when she threatened suicide. He was sympathetic when she began rejecting their adopted son. They even moved out to the suburbs in the hope that a new start would give her the boost she needed.

Nothing worked. Many years later the depression has begun to ease off, but at times it still threatens to plunge this family back into the chaos of despair. Only one – Christ – has been able to hold on to that home and bring it through. It is not a 'neat and tidy happily-ever-after story', but it's real. Through that family I have learnt that 'when all seems lost – it isn't'.

When Barbara and I got married we were sent dozens of cards. I don't remember any of them, except for the one from Martin and Pat. It was nothing out of the ordinary, but the message inside has stayed with me ever since. Beneath the printed greeting they wrote: 'The first five years are the best . . . but after that it just gets better and better.' Coming from these two people, those words had tremendous conviction and truth in them. God is faithful, and their home has proved it.

Let us accept that chaos is a normal part of everyday family life. If even Jesus's family felt it, how can we expect to avoid it? Remember that when chaos comes it is under God's control; nothing ever takes him by surprise. But when it becomes just too much for us to cope with, we must be prepared to run to Christ and hide. If you can't find a solution to the trouble, then you'll find in him someone who can carry you through.

St Paul, writing to the Christian family in Corinth, summed up all these thoughts like this:

The trials that you have had to bear are no more than people normally have. You can trust God not to let you be tried beyond your strength, and with any trial he will give you a way out of it and the strength to bear it (1 Cor. 10:13 JB).

7

CONFLICT

Conflict can be one of the richest sources of chaos in our homes, and deserves a chapter of its own. Learning to handle it properly can bring great rewards, but it isn't easy. A lot depends upon the sort of conflict we have grown up with. Let me share with you some of mine.

I learnt a lot about conflict from my parents. They loved each other but found it difficult to sort out their disagreements without creating a bit of chaos. Two incidents stand out in my memory. The first was a disagreement about the weather.

It was July 1968 and that year we had planned to go to Cornwall for a holiday. Mum and Dad had bought a caravan and stored it down by the river near where we were living. The idea of going on holiday caused great excitement and we were all looking forward to it. In the week before we were due to go, we helped Mum sort out the caravan and prepare it for the journey.

There were several warnings about heavy rain, but the floods on the Friday took us all by surprise. When I left for school that morning the river was high, but didn't look threatening. The first sign that something was wrong came when we arrived at school. There were stories of people being cut off by flood water, and one family had to be rescued by helicopter. Only half the children and teachers turned up. This was great. It meant that some lessons had to be cancelled and most of the day we had class discussions or free study.

The high point of the day was lunch. The menu was changed at the last minute due to lack of supplies, and we were all treated to strawberries and cream. This was a first (and last) for school dinners.

Meanwhile, back home the growing flood-waters had not escaped Mum's notice. At coffee-time she phoned my father to warn him that the caravan, parked next to the river, was at risk. He didn't believe her. The heavy rain had stopped by now and from where he was sitting (in an office block on top of a hill!) there was no sign of flooding. After a few well-chosen words Mum put the phone down.

When lunch-time came, the stretch of the river around the caravan burst its banks; flooding was now inevitable. She phoned the office again. Despite her description of the riverside scene, Dad refused to take any action.

By mid-afternoon it was too late. The caravan was under three feet of water, and with it our chances of a holiday in Cornwall the following week. As you might expect, this caused quite a lot of conflict in our family.

I can still remember wading through oily flood water the next day. Two of us went with Dad to try to rescue what we could from inside the caravan. The water came up to my neck in places; it was a grim exercise. Although the river had started to recede, the caravan was still flooded inside to a depth of three feet. Everything was filthy. We grabbed whatever we could carry and floated the seat cushions to shore, much to the amusement of on-lookers.

It took us a week to clean and disinfect everything. Fortunately the weather was warm and sunny and things dried out quickly. Finally, one week late, we packed up the caravan and got ready to leave for the two-hundred-mile journey south to Falmouth. The moment came to hitch the van to the car and set off: a moment I shall never forget. The water had affected the mechanism securing the towing hook on the caravan to that of the car. It was jammed fast. Two gentle taps with a hammer later and the lever broke off completely, disabling the coupling hook. A lot more conflict followed! It all started with a simple disagreement about the weather, but it turned into a storm of emotional anger which could so easily have been avoided.

Conflict that is left to grow and is not resolved can result in a flood of chaos. As we saw in the last chapter, some chaos is an inevitable part of family life. But if we let conflict get out of control it can threaten the well-being of our homes.

On another occasion my parents had a disagreement about the cooking. Mum was ill in bed and unable to make the tea. This meant that when Dad came home from work the meal wasn't ready as it usually was. For the first time in years Dad had to take charge in the kitchen.

He was quite capable of cooking but didn't take at all kindly to it. He saw his job as earning the money and Mum's job as doing everything else. Eventually, after a lot of help from his seven children, the meal was ready. We all sat down to eat. One by one the plates were brought in and set before us. It was bacon and eggs. We all had the same food. However, on Mum's plate the bacon and eggs looked somehow different. In protest at having to cook the meal, Dad had left them raw on her plate.

There was an icy silence at the table as we all began to eat. Mum, sitting at one end of the table, looked at her food and then at Dad, who sat opposite her. She said nothing. Getting up, she took the uncooked meal, walked down the room to where Dad was sitting, tipped the contents of her plate over his head and proceeded to massage the slimy egg into his hair. I think he deserved it!

This is the sort of incident good comedies are made of. It would have been a positive experience for us all if it had led to a resolution of the conflict, and Mum and Dad had hugged and kissed and made up. However, this didn't happen. The meal continued and Mum left the room.

Most of the conflict between my parents was over something trivial like the weather or the cooking. In most families it usually is. The secret is to sort out the conflict before it turns our homes into places of emotional and psychological chaos. Children can weather a lot of arguments in a family if their parents are seen to love each other in the end. Indeed conflict can be a very positive learning experience for them if it leads to a deepening of understanding between people.

Sadly, unresolved conflict builds walls of resentment between us and rivers of recriminations: '*You always ... You never*'. Bringing Christ into this situation can change things. His presence can ensure that the conflicts our families go through are creative, not destructive. We can see this from his life.

Jesus was no stranger to conflict. As we look at three episodes from the Gospels maybe one or more of them will help us to get a handle on the particular conflict we may be facing. With his help, we can turn it for good.

Episode 1: A family holiday

The first episode comes from Luke 2:41–51. This is the only account in the Bible that tells us about Jesus's childhood. This makes the incident all the more important.

In this story Jesus finds himself in conflict with his parents. It was Passover time and the whole family (uncles, aunts, friends and neighbours) had travelled down to Jerusalem for the annual celebrations. The main streets of the city were like London's Oxford Street at Christmas time. Everyone seemed to be there and it was easy to get lost in the crowds.

Mary and Joseph were used to Jesus's wandering off. He was, after all, twelve years old and at that age Jewish boys were considered to be men. The time came for the family to return to Nazareth. No one thought to check to see that Jesus was with them when they left; they all assumed he was with someone else. It was common practice for people to travel together in convoys, so Jesus was not missed during the daytime. However, when evening came and everyone bedded down for the night, Mary and Joseph began to get worried. There was no sign of him anywhere.

They went to all the tents, asking if anyone knew where he was. Not even his cousin John could give them a clue. Without waiting for daylight, the two troubled parents rushed back to Jerusalem.

When morning came, Mary and Joseph split up and began to search the different quarters of Jerusalem. They talked to some of the children they'd seen Jesus playing with. They went back to some of the taverns where they'd eaten. They looked everywhere they could think of, but there was no sign of the lost boy.

After two fruitless days of searching, Joseph was exhausted. He had a business to run in Nazareth and other children to consider. And the even greater responsibility of being a guardian of God's special Son weighed heavily upon him. He and Mary were distraught.

On the third day Joseph decided to ask some temple officials if they might know where Jesus was. It was rather embarrassing to admit that they had lost him, but by now Joseph was past caring. The main thing was to find Jesus safe and sound.

It turned out that they had been looking in the wrong place for the last two days. Jesus had found a home in the temple precincts. When they caught up with him there was a crowd of highly-qualified teachers around him deep in religious debate. He hardly noticed them when they came along and politely interrupted the exciting discussions.

Hadn't they realised where he was? Jesus was surprised. The temple was, after all, the house of his Heavenly Father and it was the logical place for him to stay when he was in Jerusalem on his own, especially now that he was a 'man'.

We aren't told much of the conversation that the two worried parents had with Jesus as they left the city that day. Those of us with children can imagine it went something like this:

Mum: Thank goodness you're safe, but where have you been? We've been worried sick. We looked everywhere for you, and started to think something awful must have happened to you. I know you're twelve now, but the big city is not a safe place for a boy your age to be alone in. There are Roman soldiers about, robbers hiding in dark corners and who knows what in some of the back-street alleys where bad women live. Anything could have happened to you!

Dad: Of course we're glad that you're safe, son. But please – don't ever do anything like that again.

Jesus beamed an innocent boyish smile at his parents, said something about 'my Father's house' which they didn't entirely understand, gave them both a big hug and told them he'd never wander off again.

And he didn't. What a wonderful son he must have been.

However, it couldn't have been easy being parents of a perfect child. Mary and Joseph are the only two people in history who have ever had this experience. Most of us think our children are perfect when they're first born, but we soon grow out of that idea as we get to know them a little better. Jesus was the exception; he was sinless – that means he never once put a foot wrong.

The same wasn't true of his parents; they were both imperfect like you and me. Yet despite this, Luke's gospel tells us that Jesus was obedient to them (Luke 2:51). This tells us something important about our relationship with our own children. If, as a child, Jesus chose to obey parents who were not perfect when he was, we should have no qualms in teaching our children to do the same – yes, even if we think they are perfect!

Obedience

The Bible doesn't tell us how many children we should have. It doesn't tell us what to dress our children in or feed them with. It doesn't say whether it's right or wrong to send our children to private schools. But its teaching about childhood obedience could not be clearer.

St Paul bases his teaching about this on the fifth commandment in Exodus 20, verse 12: 'Honour your father and your mother, so that you may live long in the land the LORD your God is giving you.' To the Christians at Ephesus he wrote: 'Children, obey your parents in the Lord, for this is right' (Eph. 6:1); and again, to the Christians at Colossae he said: 'Children, obey your parents in everything, for this pleases the Lord' (Col. 3:20).

Obedience is an area of great conflict for parents. I do not know of a single parent who has taught their children to disobey them. But I know a lot of parents who have trouble with their children disobeying them. There are good scriptural reasons for this trend in human nature. The first parents passed this family characteristic on to the first children, Cain and Abel, and it has been inherited ever since.

We should not be surprised, therefore, when our children disobey us. They are only doing what it is in their nature to do. Children are born with a desire to rebel because of the consequences of Genesis 3. This takes us back to 'paradise lost' and the reasons for human sin that we looked at in chapter 2.

When it comes to facing conflict in the home, the life of Jesus shows us that not even 'perfect' children are exempt from obeying their parents. Perhaps the Holy Spirit caused Luke to include this episode from the life of Jesus to make a point for all future parents: 'Even when you feel a failure as a parent and blame yourself for the way your children have turned out, don't let them off the hook. They must learn obedience from you.'

There are very good reasons for this. If our children learn to do what we tell them when they are growing up, they will be learning to obey those in authority over them. This will prepare them for adult life in two ways.

First, as members of society they will find it easier to obey the laws of the land. Second, as children of God they will find it easier to obey someone they can't see, when they have learnt to obey someone they can.

The writer of Proverbs says, 'Train a child in the way he should go, and when he is old he will not turn from it' (Prov. 22:6). This principle works both ways. If we teach children to obey, then as they grow up obedience will be part of their make-up as people; it will be in their character to obey. If we don't teach children to obey, then as they grow up they will have disobedience written into their character. Disobedience will become a dominating force in their lives which may result in disaster for them, their family and the society around them.

Many of the problems I come across in ministry are caused by conflict in this area. People who have not learnt obedience in their childhood find it very hard to obey God when as adults they seek to follow Christ. We do not do children any favours by giving in to them; we only teach them that obedience is a matter of convenience and leave them exposed to more temptation than they would otherwise have to face.

The obedience I am referring to is not meant to be a tyranny of one person manipulating and controlling another. True scriptural obedience is very different to this. It is the willing desire of one person to submit himself in love to another. It is not an easy virtue to learn or to teach, because it goes against the grain of our human nature to obey anyone. By nature we are all born rebels.

Submissive spirit

In our kitchen we have a 'jobs' list. It's been on the go for about five or six years now. We started it as a way of helping the children to learn to do chores around the house 'willingly', without Mum or Dad ordering them about.

We all sat down together to draw up the list. Everyone had a chance to suggest jobs that needed doing: emptying the bins, cleaning out the hamster cage, washing, vacuuming, table-laying, and so on. Once the list was finished we talked about who should do what – Mum and Dad were included on the list to make it as fair as possible. Then everyone was slotted into place. We decided Saturday, my day off, should be an 'all-hands-on-deck' sort of day, with everyone mucking in (or, as happens sometimes, Mum and Dad doing everything!).

From the very first day we started this scheme, a miracle happened in our house. The children started to do the jobs around the house without arguing. They had agreed the order of play; they could see what the list said and no one could say, 'It's not fair', because the jobs had been shared out equally.

As the plan got going we started to review it. Was everyone happy with their jobs? Would they like to swap? Were there any jobs that had been left out? There were minor changes from time to time. When the rota had been going for some time I asked our eldest son to swap the jobs around so that people would get the chance to do things on different days. He talked to his brothers and sister about some of the changes, and we agreed to carry on.

For several years this 'jobs-list' has worked wonders, and until recently I thought it had taken most of the chaos out of this area of conflict in the home. However, I was mistaken. It seems that though the children were keeping to the letter of the jobs list they were rebelling against the spirit of it. The idea had been to reach co-operation in the home and a sense of responsibility. But gradually it's become clear to me that this has not been happening.

Things came to a head when I was away from home for three months on study leave. My absence during the week (we were together at weekends) meant one less person to do the jobs around the house. This put the system under a strain. It also meant that at weekends there was a backlash. Saturday, which had traditionally been an 'everyone helps' day, became a 'I'm not doing it this week, I did it last time' day.

The cause of the problem was not just my temporary absence and the increased work load it placed on everyone else. The deeper reason was an unwillingness to submit and serve someone else in love.

We haven't abandoned the jobs list because at the moment we can't think of anything better to replace it. But we now must insist that no one goes to watch television, to do their homework or out to play until all the jobs have been properly finished. Everyone is asked to share the burden and responsibiities of others, as far as they are able.

We don't yet know what the outcome of this will be. But in principle I believe this sort of scheme is right for families. However, my failure to teach our children to obey from their hearts willingly and in love has given me a lot to think and pray about. For me the only true obedience that matters is one from the heart; it is what St Paul meant when he said children should obey 'in the Lord' and to 'please the Lord'. To teach true obedience is to cultivate in our children a willing spirit of submission; the Bible does not give parents the right to be tyrants.

Smacking

Those of us who use smacking to discipline our children need to be very careful how we read the Scriptures in this respect; Bible verses such as:

> He who spares the rod hates his son, but he who loves him is careful to discipline him (Prov. 13:2).

> Folly is bound up in the heart of a child, but the rod of discipline will drive it far from him (Prov. 22:15).

> Do not withhold discipline from a child; if you punish him with the rod he will not die. Punish him with the rod and save his soul from death (Prov. 23:13–14).

> The rod of correction imparts wisdom, but a child left to itself disgraces his mother (Prov. 29:15).

need to be set against other verses such as:

> Fathers, do not exasperate your children; instead, bring them up in the training and instruction of the Lord (Eph. 6:4).

> Fathers, do not provoke your children, lest they become discouraged (Col. 3:21 RSV).

need to be set alongside the teaching of Jesus in the Gospels about children:

> Jesus said, 'Let the little children come to me, and do not hinder them, for the kingdom of heaven belongs to such as these' (Matt. 19:14; also Mark 10:13–16 and Luke 18:15–16).

Things that cause people to sin are bound to come, but woe to that person through whom they come. It would be better for him to be thrown into the sea with a millstone tied round his neck than for him to cause one of these little ones to sin. So watch yourselves (Luke 17:1–3).

I have found myself justifying smacking with some of the references above from Proverbs. But nowhere does the Bible say that obedience can or should be beaten into a child. The aim of all forms of discipline in the home must be to bring our children to obey and love God. We should teach them to obey us so that they can obey God, not so we can control and manipulate them.

Solomon's concern in Proverbs about the behaviour of children may well have been caused by what he saw happen to his half-brother Adonijah. 1 Kings 1:6 tells us that David didn't discipline this son. He also appears to have spoilt his elder brother Absalom. Both these children grew up to be terrible rebels and betrayed David.

Whatever form of discipline we use in training our children, we need to make the principle of obedience our top priority. For it is at the heart of what it means to know and love God: 'If you love me you will obey what I command' (John 14:15).

Jesus learnt obedience 'through what he suffered' (Heb. 5:8 RSV). This included the suffering he must have experienced through being brought up by two imperfect parents. Don't be afraid to keep working at obedience in your home. When children are obedient they are conforming to how Jesus behaved and how God made them to be.

Episode 2   A family tug-of-war

In Matthew 12:46–50 Jesus found himself in conflict with his family. He was well into his ministry by this stage. His teaching on the hill top overlooking Lake Galilee had already become legendary.

However, Jesus seemed to be taken over by the demands of

the crowds. He exhausted himself in healing, made his name headline news by driving out demons, and got into trouble with the religious 'heavy mob' by saying uncomfortable things that they didn't want to hear.

The net result was that his family couldn't get near him. He didn't know why they were so keen to speak to him on that particular day. Maybe they'd heard rumours that the village elders were ganging up on him, and wanted to protect him. Perhaps they were scared of what was going to happen to him if he carried on his ministry like this. Whatever the reason, they sent word that they had arrived and asked him to stop his work for the moment so they could speak to him.

This was probably one of many occasions when Jesus found himself in a tug-of-war situation. On the one hand his family knew and loved him; they'd had him to themselves for thirty years and still wanted his attention. His work was taking him farther and farther away from them and they probably resented the crowds who now monopolised him instead.

On the other hand, ever since he had been baptised and come back from the six-weeks' struggle in the wilderness, Jesus knew that he must devote himself entirely to his public ministry. Other things like safety, comfort, food and even his own family must take second place.

The message Jesus sent back to his mother and brothers sounded hurtful: 'Who is my mother, and who are my brothers? . . . For whoever does the will of my Father in heaven is my brother and sister and mother' (Matt. 12:48, 50). And it probably upset them all when they got it. But Jesus was making an important point to them, the crowd and to us: when there is a conflict of loyalties in our relationships, what God wants must always come first.

This is not a popular spiritual principle. It causes emotional conflict in marriages, especially when one partner is not a Christian. It makes decisions about how we spend our time and money more difficult. It brings us into conflict with well-meaning relatives and friends who wonder why we think worship on a Sunday is more important than going out for a birthday picnic.

It will bring us into conflict in our place of work when our employer demands we do overtime on a Sunday, or expects us to do things that are illegal or immoral.

From a human point of view, it seems a very bad option indeed. The temptation to 'go with the flow' is very powerful, especially in a society like ours which has slipped its moral moorings. In love, but with complete conviction, we need to dig in and hold our ground in these tug-of-war situations. It may hurt. It will certainly be costly. But the alternative is to slide farther and farther away from what God wants us to be.

Jason's story

Jason was a sales rep for a successful company, and had helped open up a number of new outlets for the company product. Everything was going well for him at the firm until his boss told him to take over a new account.

From the moment he started to check the sales figures, he could tell that there were irregularities. Something was seriously wrong. The volume of sales recorded for the last three years did not tally with the turnover quoted in the accounts for the same period. In effect, a percentage of company profits had simply 'disappeared' from the accounts. The profit margin had been incorrectly quoted, so as to conceal the theft.

When he took the matter up with his boss, he was encouraged to 'look again'. This was a polite way of telling him to mind his own business. He was being asked to turn a blind eye to the discrepancies.

Jason found himself in a tug-of-war situation. As a Christian he knew what he was being asked to do was wrong. God did not want him to lie about the figures when they were presented to the stockholders or to pretend somehow that the problem didn't exist. On the other hand he needed his job. He had a mortgage, two growing children and a disabled wife. He could not afford to be out of work.

He shared the problem with me and we prayed. The next day he told his boss that unless he was given some explanation about the distortion in the sales figures, he would report the matter to the board of directors. After a rather unpleasant scene, the manager concerned took him off the account and in effect downgraded him. There followed a very unpleasant few weeks. Getting up for work on a Monday morning was unusually difficult, but at least he still had a job.

Later that year the company underwent a major restructuring process. Jason, who had given many years of faithful service, put in hours of unpaid overtime, and had never been late for work in his life found himself out of a job. The explanation given was 'streamlining' of certain departments. The truth was that Jason had become an embarrassment. He was also a potential risk to those in his company who were 'massaging' the sales figures and creaming off company profits into their own private investment fund.

Jason and his family were devastated at the redundancy. Who had won in this tug-of-war? At forty-nine Jason found it difficult to get another job. He was 'too old' or 'too well-qualified' or 'not fresh enough' for most of the jobs he applied for. The decision to stand his ground was right, but the consequences were hard to bear. He had done what was right in God's sight but it looked as though his family would suffer most because of it.

As the weeks turned into months of unemployment Jason began to wonder whether he had made the right decision after all. Could God mean for his wife and children to suffer like this for the sake of Christian principles? Despite his strong faith, the cracks began to show.

His wife and children were wonderful. They didn't understand all the 'ins-and-outs' of this unhappy conflict, but gave him all the love and moral support that they could. The suffering of those months brought them all closer than they had ever been before. Despite the drastic drop in income, God was providing for them.

Eventually God in his faithfulness brought Jason and his family through. Eighteen months later he got a job with a new EC firm which had just opened up an outlet in Edinburgh and wanted him to help establish its sales force. It meant moving house and schools, but the new job was better paid and allowed him the flexibility to be at home looking after his wife when she needed special care. What's more it didn't require him to break the law in order to earn a living. It even meant his two teenage sons got near enough to Glenshee to learn to ski properly.

Not all tug-of-war stories end like this, of course. But in the providence and faithfulness of God, he never allows us to be put to shame when we do what is right in his eyes. As Psalm 25 puts it:

> To you, O LORD, I lift up my soul; in you I trust, O my God. Do not let me be put to shame, nor let my enemies triumph over me. No-one whose hope is in you will ever be put to shame, but they will be put to shame who are treacherous without excuse (vv. 1–3).

Helen's story

Helen's tug-of-war was a little different. Her father was gay. No one knew about it until after she had left home and got married. He was often away from home when she was little, but her mother had always told her it was business. Some of it was; but for many years her father had been secretly committing adultery with various men. None of the affairs lasted very long, and after they were over he would try to make it up to her mother. But in the end it proved too much. When Helen's first child was born her mother announced that she was getting a divorce.

Meanwhile, her father had moved into a flat with a male partner. When she realised what was going on, Helen was devastated. At first she couldn't believe it. She loved her father and insisted on getting his side of the story.

When he came to see her one night she broke down in tears. This sort of thing happened in books or on television, but not in your own family. Her father told her everything. He asked her to try to understand that this gay life-style didn't change the way he felt about her or about his first grandchild. He hoped that in time she would accept his 'boyfriend' too, because they had committed themselves to each other and written a sort of marriage contract.

The visit actually made things worse for a while. When her mother first broke the news to her Helen thought that this was just a 'phase' her father was going through. She'd read about latent homosexuality in books and thought that once he'd got these feelings out of his system he would be 'normal' again. The mention of the word 'marriage' and 'joint wills' soon cured her of that idea.

For months after the visit, Helen refused to speak to her father or have anything to do with him. She completely cut herself off from him. The divorce had been very messy and her mother didn't encourage her to do anything about this broken relationship.

When Helen's husband Mark announced one day that he was up for promotion, which meant moving to the other side of the country, Helen felt relieved. By putting distance between herself and her father she no longer needed to face the conflict that was raging inside her. The move couldn't have happened at a better time. Or so she thought.

A few months later, having settled into a new area, Helen came to see me. She was depressed. The doctor had given her medication and put it down to post-natal causes. But as we talked together the trauma over her parents' divorce rose to the surface.

It was many weeks before Helen could speak about her father civilly. All her resentment was directed towards what he had done, how he had hurt her mother and deprived his only grandchild of a 'proper' grandparents' home. To make matters worse, her father was supposed to be a committed Christian. She was revolted and disgusted by what he had done.

In time we looked at the Bible together. As I read Romans 1:18–32 I asked her to tell me how much of this she thought applied to her father. Was he someone who rejected the 'knowledge of God' (v. 28); was he 'evil', 'greedy', 'depraved' (v. 29); a 'gossiper, slanderer, God-hater ...' (v. 30)? Long before we reached the end of the list she broke down in tears. No, despite what her father was doing there were many things about him that she still loved and that were wholly good. Cutting him off in the way she had done more than damaged their relationship. It was also hurting Helen very deeply inside and had caused the depression to take hold.

That Christmas, Helen and Mark steeled themselves to visit her father. They travelled over to see him at New Year. They exchanged presents, met his boyfriend, and even had a meal in his flat. She promised Mark she wouldn't say anything in public to embarrass her father. In private, while she helped her father with the washing up, she told him of her feelings about the way he was living. There was some straight talking, quite a few icy silences and finally a lot of tears as they hugged each other in a father-daughter grip.

Since then Helen and Mark have made regular visits to see her father and sometimes stayed with him too. There was a difficult moment when they were offered the double bed where her father and his boyfriend normally slept, but remembering how Jesus loved 'those who needed a physician' they took a deep breath and agreed. Her father often comes to stay with them now and usually is not alone. Mark insists that they sleep in different rooms while they are there, but this has usually been accepted with good humour.

This tug-of-war situation does not have a tidy ending. Ten years on, Helen is still unhappy with the way her father lives and finds it difficult to explain to her three children why their grandad lives with their 'uncle' and not with grandma. But she has found an openness and depth in her relationship with her father that she never had before. In time she hopes that he will be set free from the grip of this particular sin. In the meantime she has promised to get to work on some of her own!

It is no coincidence that St Paul follows his teaching about sexual immorality in Romans chapter 1 with the words: 'You therefore, have no excuse, you who pass judgment on someone else . . .' at the beginning of chapter 2. As Jesus himself put it in that timeless story from John 8: 'If any one of you is without sin, let him be the first to throw a stone . . .' (v. 7).

When family conflicts bring us into a tug-of-war situation, we need to grasp the truth in one hand and the love of Christ in the other. Truth without love will turn us into Pharisees; love without truth will turn us into jellyfish. In Matthew 12:49 we saw how Jesus told his family the truth. It upset them. Maybe they even had a family row. Yet in the very next chapter, we find him back home with them again as if to emphasise the fact that he still loved them. Truth and love. Jesus held these two things together perfectly in his life as we shall see in this third episode from the Gospels.

Episode 3   A lost cause?

Every year the words from Matthew 27:46 stop me in my tracks: 'My God, my God, why have you forsaken me?' During a recent series of Holy Week vigils I found myself frequently in tears as I considered what these words meant for Jesus.

All his life Jesus had served other people. Even when he was born, the precious gift of gold from one of the wise men made sure that his family wouldn't have to flee to Egypt destitute. Jesus affected everyone he met for good.

He had carried away the cares and shame of an outcast, rejected woman (Matt. 9:20–2). He had put language and sight back into the bodies of medically hopeless cases (Matt. 9:27–33). He had raised from death a family friend whose last will and testament had long since been read (John 11:1–44). He'd even risked his life by touching a man with a serious skin disease (Matt. 8:3), much to the amazement of those who watched him do it.

Yet, here he was at the end of his life totally alone. There were one or two of his disciples around. John had stayed with his mother Mary for as long as she could bear it and had then taken her, utterly distraught, to his own home. A few women whose lives had been totally changed by his incredible love had stood at a distance where his naked, tortured body would not embarrass them.

Jesus had never failed anyone; now he watched as his own

body failed to withstand the horrors of this cruel method of execution. How could God the Father possibly forsake his one and only Son? How could Jesus himself suffer this treatment that he neither deserved nor desired?

Only on the Monday of that week, with formidable authority over creation, he had turned a leafy fig-tree into a withering stump (Matt. 21:18–19). Why did he not now turn the terrible cross he was on into a sword and destroy those who had pinned him to it?

The mystery of Golgotha is something that none of us can ever fully understand. But its message of hope echoes through history. There is hope for every marriage, every parent, every child and every family where Christ is allowed to enter in. When you and I welcome Jesus into our marriages, our families, the places where we live and work, we are welcoming someone who has championed the greatest lost cause in the world and turned the apparent victory of evil into the promise of its eternal defeat.

Jesus emptied the bottom out of human God-forsakenness by dying on the cross for our sin. The reason Jesus chose to allow himself to be cut off from God and die a criminal's death was so that we might escape the experience of feeling abandoned by God. The Bible says 'All have sinned and fall short of the glory of God' (Rom. 3:23), and 'Everyone has turned away . . . there is no one who does good, not even one' (Ps. 53:3), and 'Sin entered the world through one man, and death through sin, and in this way death came to all men, because all sinned' (Rom. 5:12).

Things may get pretty bad in our homes at times, but it is never right to describe them as God-forsaken. Christ came to deal with our feelings of desolation; his abandonment on the cross achieved a wonderful exchange: our sin for his life, our mistakes for his victory, our sorrows for his joy. As St Peter puts it: 'He himself bore our sins in his body on the tree, so that we might die to sins and live for righteousness' and then he adds those amazing words, 'by his wounds you have been healed' (Pet. 2:24).

These are staggering words. If they are true it means that there is no such thing as a lost cause in our homes. Are our teenagers impossibly rebellious? Christ died to deal with the causes of their sin. Have our toddlers driven us to despair with their terrible tantrums and iron-hard wills? Christ came to overcome the consequences of their sin. Do we look back on the way we've brought our children up and feel failures at the way they've turned out? Christ came to redeem human children like yours and mine from their sin.

Because of the work of Calvary, there is no such thing as a lost cause. 'Everything is possible for him who believes' (Mark 9:23) – words spoken by Jesus to a father who had virtually written off his son as a 'lost cause'. Jesus changed all that; he seemed especially interested in lost causes. That's why he's so concerned for you and me!

As I found myself weeping during one of the vigils in Holy Week, Jesus reminded me of what Psalm 22:1 led to. Breathing was agony for a crucified victim and the first verse was the only part of the psalm Jesus had the strength to utter aloud. But perhaps in his head he went farther.

The psalm goes on to describe the sort of pain and agony that Jesus had to go through. But it is immediately followed by those wonderful words of hope in the next psalm: 'The Lord is my shepherd, I shall lack nothing' (Ps. 23:1). And then those fabulous words in the next psalm: 'Lift up your heads, O you gates; be lifted up, you ancient doors, that the King of Glory may come in' (Ps. 24:7).

Golgotha didn't conclude with forsakenness, it ended with a triumphant cry of victory: 'It is finished' (John 19:30). When Jesus bowed down his head and died, he put an end to all lost causes, once and for all.

8

MONEY WORRIES

My grandmother used to say, 'When poverty comes in the door, love flies out the window.' She was talking about getting married when you're poor. To fall in love is one thing: but to be married without money is another.

Barbara and I had the chance to test this saying out from our second day of marriage. It was a Sunday. We had travelled by coach from Birmingham and had arrived at our Keswick destination just before 10 p.m. The journey hadn't started too well. When we boarded the coach, we found (to our dismay) that there were only single seats left. Here we were, newly married, facing a seven-hour coach journey sitting apart.

Moving up and down the aisle I eventually plucked up courage to ask someone if they would mind moving. As it happened, the two people I asked were a married couple. They were sitting in separate seats one behind the other, so that they could 'spread out'. When I explained our situation they were more than happy to oblige. We thanked them and settled down for the long journey to one of our favourite destinations.

The Lake District held many happy memories for us. It was the place where God had first brought us together in friendship and then later in love. We were thrilled to be able to spend our first days of marriage together in this most beautiful place.

However, the thrill of being in Keswick rapidly evaporated when we got off the coach. The driver went to get our luggage and handed me Barbara's suitcase. Then he handed me another. It wasn't mine. In fact it didn't belong to anyone left on the coach. My suitcase had mysteriously disappeared.

What a start to married life. All my clothes and our bedding for the flat we were renting were in my suitcase, together with all my toiletries – including the packet of condoms that it contained! As the biting rain of a Cumbrian April evening drove into my face, I felt well and truly 'gutted'.

The coach driver was very apologetic and suggested we take the spare case and return to the bus station the next day to sort something out. There didn't seem much alternative but to take his advice. We climbed into the taxi waiting to take us to our honeymoon destination in Bassenthwaite.

Somehow the excitement of being married had evaporated. We had no sheets or sex to look forward to that night. Fortunately the couple renting us the flat were very sympathetic when we poured out our tale of woe. They lent us some sheets for the bed (the sex had to wait) and then suggested we should open the case to see if there were any clues about who it belonged to. Thus began a long saga which continued throughout the honeymoon.

When we opened the case, on top of the clothes was a passport. It didn't have an address, but it told us the name of the owner: he came from Morecambe. When we saw his picture we could hardly believe our eyes. This was the man who had given up his seat for us at Birmingham so we could sit together for the journey! We had a good laugh about it, especially when we pictured how he must have felt when he opened my suitcase that day and found it was stuffed full of confetti.

The next day the man behind the counter at the bus depot in Keswick looked at us in astonishment as we told him what had happened. He too had a good laugh about it all and then promised he would do his best to find out what had happened to our case. We left to enjoy a day in one of our favourite towns, expecting we would hear by the end of the day that my case was on its way north.

Monday came and went with no news. Tuesday morning I phoned through to Keswick from the bungalow. Was there any news? 'No, sir, I'm sorry but we haven't heard anything yet.' The mystery deepened.

Surely if the man from Morecambe had got my suitcase he would realise at once that it wasn't his. He knew that we were going on honeymoon to Keswick and although my name wasn't in my suitcase, the confetti in it would tell him all he needed to know. We went into Keswick on the bus again, hoping for more news. Nothing.

By this time walking about in a pin-striped suit was beginning to wear a little thin. I had already had to buy underclothes the day before and would soon need to think about something more substantial to change into.

Tuesday came and went with still no news. By Wednesday we concluded that the suitcase had been stolen, and reported this to the police. Meanwhile, for the third day running we travelled into Keswick, resigned to the fact that all my clothes had gone for good.

It was lunch-time by the time we got into town. And in those days many of the shops were shut on Wednesday afternoons, including the shop where I had planned to buy some clothes. This honeymoon was beginning to turn into a nightmare.

We had come to the Lakes hoping to do some walking; there was snow on the top of Skiddaw and walks to it from our front door in Bassenthwaite. But climbing a mountain in a pin-striped suit is not such a good idea. That afternoon we returned once more to the bus depot and filled out an insurance claim form. At least I would get a new wardrobe of clothes out of all this hassle.

This whole incident had cast a shadow over our first few days of married life. How could God have allowed this to happen? What was he trying to tell us? We had spent everything we had on the wedding preparations, reception and honeymoon. The clothes I had in the suitcase represented my entire wardrobe; there was nothing at all left in the flat at home in Gillingham. Where had the suitcase gone? Why had the man from More-cambe not got it!? 'When poverty comes in the door . . .' those words kept coming back to me during those days of honeymoon.

As we talked, laughed, prayed and (yes) cried about the situation I realised that this event so early on in our home life together was no accident. This was God speaking to me through my money worries. It had been a real financial struggle to save up for the wedding, find a reasonable flat to rent, buy basic furniture for it, and still have money left over to spend on the honeymoon. By the time we got to Keswick we were virtually broke. Would 'the Lord provide' for us in this situation, or was it up to us to get ourselves out of this mess?

This is an important question that all of us need to come to terms with in our homes and families. All of us will have times in our lives when the money runs out or when unexpected disasters happen. We may suddenly be made redundant. We may be just managing to pay the mortgage when the interest rates shoot up. The car goes in for a routine repair and then comes back with a four-figure bill. At some stage in our family life an economic storm or earthquake will strike: what do you do when it does? What difference does it make to bring Christ into our money worries?

In Jesus's Sermon on the Mount he taught his followers a basic principle to help us in our struggles with money worries: 'do not worry about your life, what you will eat or drink; or about your body, what you will wear. Is not life more important than food, and the body more important than clothes?' he said (Matt. 6:25).

Jesus knew what it was like to be hard up. He began life as a refugee. His family wasn't wealthy. He had no salary to live on when he began his public ministry. And yet we find him with gold in his hand when he was a baby (Matt. 2:11) and food in his stomach when everyone else was starving (John 4:32). He was accused of lack of self-control when he dined with wealthy and greedy people (Matt. 9:11), and provided money for others out of nowhere (Matt. 17:27; Luke 5:5–6). What was his secret for living life to the full without ever worrying about money?

The answer lies in that little word 'therefore' which comes at the beginning of Matthew 6:25. The principle of worry-less living was based on three things.

1   Sound money

Do not store up for yourselves treasures on earth, where moth and rust destroy, and where thieves break in and steal. But store up for yourselves treasures in heaven, where moth and rust do not destroy, and where thieves do not break in and steal. For where your treasure is, there your heart will be also (Matt. 6:19–21).

The point Jesus was making is very simple. If moths don't eat your clothes, then changing fashions will soon mean those lovely flares are definitely out. If rust doesn't one day bring your car to a halt, then mechanical failure certainly will. If burglars don't relieve you of your hard-earned savings, then inflation will eventually destroy their value instead. What does the economic future hold? None of us knows. But of one thing we can be certain: the future of this world is decline and decay. His advice to people is therefore to make spiritual investments in heaven instead. We'll have a look in a moment about what this means in practice.

2   Sound vision

The eye is the lamp of the body. If your eyes are good, your whole body will be full of light. But if your eyes are bad, your whole body will be full of darkness. If then the light within you is darkness, how great is that darkness! (Matt. 6:22–3).

When I put glasses on for the first time I felt as if a miracle had taken place. As I left the opticians and looked down the road, the number plates of cars and signs of shops in the distance suddenly came into sharp focus. I didn't need glasses in order to see the cars; my eyesight wasn't that bad. But wearing the glasses made it possible for me to see detail more clearly; I began noticing things which I hadn't seen before.

Bringing Christ into our money worries has this effect on t way we see our income; he helps us to look at things differen

Focusing on the wrong things in life will make us short-sighed.
Jesus wanted us to look beyond the immediate to the long term.

Bad eyesight doesn't usually come overnight; it usually creeps
up on us year by year. The same can be true when it comes to
worrying about money. Problems with our income usually begin
with bad patterns of behaviour which have happened over a long
period of time. When Christ comes into the situation he brings
these into sharp focus, helping us to see the problems for what
they really are. His Spirit at work in us can help to correct our
vision and help us see things differently.

3   Sound attitudes

No-one can serve two masters. Either he will hate the one and
love the other, or he will be devoted to the one and despise
the other. You cannot serve both God and Money (Matt 6:24).

My father used to own a small supermarket. I worked in it for six
months before I started teaching. The best time of day was when
it was busy. The clatter of the cash register, the clink of the off-
licence, the shuffling past the customers to dash upstairs for
more supplies . . . Activity seemed to make the day go better.

But however much I tried, it was impossible to serve two
people at once. If someone wanted some meat from the butchery
department I couldn't fetch some more potatoes for someone
else from the stock room. If I was selling someone their
Christmas supply of booze, I couldn't be on the till checking-out
other customers. I had to make a choice.

The same thing applies to our attitudes towards money. When
we go to work each day, do we do it for the money, or for God?
When we buy a house does money dictate the size, shape and
position of the property? Or do we ask God's advice about
finding the best place? When we plan our spending on food,
clothing, holidays, presents and other things, does the bank
balance control how we live, what luxuries we indulge in, and
how much we give away? Or does everything come down to what
we hear God say?

Jesus said that you can't have it both ways. You must choose whether money or God will be your master. The choice which you and I make will decide whether we end up worrying about food bills, clothing costs, mortgage rates, inflation figures ... or not.

Let me suggest three ways Christ can help us with our money worries.

Christ helps us to face the truth

If we want to escape from money worries, we need to be truthful with God about how money affects us. I have found this a constant battle – money is subject to rapid truth decay.

However much I pretend to myself that I'm trusting God for my money supply at the beginning of the month, by the time the bank statement's come and I've worked out how much is left after all the out-goings, the truth is that I often don't. It only takes the arrival of a few unexpected bills to make me say, 'Help! Where's the money going to come from to pay for this one?'

Our car is usually the thing that exposes the truth. A few months ago it began making rattling noises. During a routine service the garage told me that there was a problem with the gearbox. They assured me that it would probably last for quite a while, but one of the mechanics advised me to get rid of the car before the problem got worse. For various reasons this wasn't a practical option, so instead we prayed.

During the next few weeks the problem got much worse. We prayed harder – more out of desperation than faith. Finally the grinding noise in the gearbox brought the car to a complete standstill. When the breakdown vehicle arrived the mechanic told me not to get my hopes up; it looked pretty bad. A few minutes later the car was on its way to the most expensive repair bill of its life (and mine).

The next day I took a deep breath, telephoned the garage and asked them what the verdict was on my car. 'Are you sitting down, sir?' said a voice at the other end of the telephone.

'Is it that bad?' I asked, hoping and praying that it wasn't.

'I'm afraid it is. Your engine needs a new gearbox.' This was the worst-case scenario. I had hoped that it would be something a little less expensive. With labour, parts and all the little 'extras' the final total came to £1,146.51. I sat down for quite a long time after that.

How do you respond to a repair bill like that? Trust God for the money? Truthfully? When I finished my conversation with the garage mechanic, I felt a sick feeling inside of me as I thought of the money that this metal monster was about to demand from me.

This was the week before we were due to go away for our summer holiday. The cottage we had planned to stay in still needed to be paid for. In addition to this we had to find resources to pay for a new uniform and equipment, as Samuel was about to move from junior to secondary school. The four-figure bill for the car repair couldn't have arrived at a worse time. It tested my faith in God's ability to provide for us to the utmost limit.

I looked at our money supply and concluded that it was beyond our means to meet all our commitments. As I wrestled with these money worries I began to realise that I was trusting more in my own resources than in the resources of almighty God, whom the Bible calls 'Jehovah-Jireh': the Lord will provide (Gen. 22:14).

From an early stage in our home together, Barbara and I discovered money worries made our trust in God quickly evaporate. So we decided to do something about it. We began a weekly 'prayer of faith' dairy. Each weekend we would discuss what this 'prayer of faith' should be. It had to be a short-term prayer request, something that could reasonably be answered by God in the week ahead. It needed to be something tangible and measurable – 'God bless the world' type prayers were out.

Above all it had to be something which was within our threshold of faith. By this I mean that the prayer had to be a request that we believed God could meet. Truth was a very important part of this 'faith-building' exercise in our family life. We had to be sure before we agreed on the prayer request for the week ahead, that we could truthfully say to God, 'Lord, we believe that you can do this ... please grant our request!' This also meant being sure that what we asked for wasn't the sort of prayer God was unlikely to answer – 'God give me a million pounds, and make it quick' prayers were simply not on!

We began this weekly routine in a very simply way. There were prayers such as: 'Father, please help us to wake up on time this week'; 'Lord, give us the strength to cope with x and y at school'; 'Please, Jesus, bring a new person to the missionary prayer meeting on Wednesday.' Week by week we kept a diary of these prayers, and at the end of the week checked to see if the prayer of faith had been answered.

They always were, and this encouraged us to step out farther in faith. We began to be more specific in our prayers: 'Lord, please send good weather on Tuesday for the games lesson we've got planned'; 'Father, please send us news from our friends in Thailand this week'; 'Please Lord, give us some special encouragement in our work at school this week.' This in turn led us on to become bolder and bolder in our prayers.

Again, looking back on all of these prayers, God proved himself amazingly trustworthy. Nearly all were answered within the given period of time. However, this sort of trust in God cannot be stored up; it soon evaporates if you don't keep on truthfully servicing your relationship with God in this area.

Whenever I come to the point (as I did with the car bill) of doubting that God can be trusted to provide for us it is usually because I have allowed my level of trust in him to deteriorate. Bringing Christ into our money worries means being prepared to take action to do something about our level of trust.

In his Sermon on the Mount Jesus challenged his followers about their money and material worries (Matt. 6:25–34). This wasn't because he wanted to make people feel embarrassed or ashamed. He never did that to people. His concern was to help people to trust God for all their daily needs; he wants to do the same for us today.

Christ helps us to budget

My first experience of working out a family budget was in our first year at theological college. I had applied for a local authority grant for the three-year training course but was unsuccessful. This left us in a dilemma. We had no money saved; no house to sell or rent in order to provide some capital to live on; Barbara was expecting our second child and too busy with a year-old baby even to think about going back to work. Our home church was unable to help us, and the church authorities made it clear that being 'recommended for training' was conditional on being able to provide for my family.

My college tuition fees were paid for and a small amount left over just about covered a term's rent. But by the end of October we were in serious financial difficulty. I believed God had called me to leave teaching and train for ministry in the Church of England. Yet I had no resources of my own to support my family while I trained.

At the beginning of November I went to see my college principal. He was very supportive and told me not to worry. After telling him about our financial crisis he gave me a grant-loan of £200 and sent me away with a budget form to complete.

The money helped, but the budget form frightened me to death. I had never sat down and worked out, item by item, how much everything we needed would cost. I hardly knew where to begin. Fortunately, Barbara is a much better accountant than I am and together we got started. By the time we had finished my fear turned to hysterical laughter.

There was no way that we were ever going to meet the target figures for all the budgeted items. We went through the figures again. Could we cut down on food items? Were holidays for the foreseeable future 'impossible'? Should we do without new clothes and live on jumble sales and charity shops? We went through every option but at the end of the day we still had a budget deficit of thousands of pounds.

This only confirmed what I felt from the start: we should never have enough money from all available resources to keep us at college. For the next month we lived on the grant-loan, waited and prayed. Three people living on fifty pounds a week was an interesting experience. By the time heating, lighting, a few essential books, nappies and a whole variety of 'sundries' were taken out of this, there wasn't much left in the bank for food.

We managed to survive like this until the second week in December. The 'prayer of faith' we had been keeping up all this time was beginning to get a little desperate by now. There wasn't any need to discuss what the entry in our prayer diary should be each week: 'Lord, give us this day our daily bread' was roughly how it ran.

On 7 December I began the week with a choice. It was time to stop trusting in my resources and start believing in the Lord. The items on our budget weren't luxuries. They were what amounted to 'our daily bread'. We had come to a crossroads. Either we had made a mistake and disobeyed God in leaving a secure career to train for ministry; I should therefore give up college and go back into teaching. Or we were in the right place, doing what God had called us to do and should simply trust that he would provide.

On Monday evening Barbara and I talked this through and decided that we must put our budget needs to the ultimate test. At our wedding ceremony we had sung: 'Great is thy faithfulness, O God my Father, there is no shadow of turning with thee. Thou changest not, thy compassions they fail not. As thou has been thou wilt surely remain: Great is thy faithfulness' (words based on Lam. 3:23). Now it was time to see whether we really believed it.

On the following day, Tuesday, I decided to fast (not very difficult under the circumstances) and pray, consciously bringing Christ into this situation and laying the matter before him. As I met with Jesus, three things happened.

a) I felt his assurance that we were in the right place and should stay put.
b) I experienced a deep sense of peace that I hadn't had about this money worry for many weeks.

c) I heard an almost audible voice say to me: 'Use what I have
   already given you.'

This last idea took me a bit by surprise. In all my worrying about
providing for my family I hadn't actually done a stock-take in the
kitchen. We had used up everything in the bank, but as we
looked in the cupboards we began to grow in faith.

It's surprising when you survey your larder how many tins
have escaped your notice. The cupboards weren't full and they
didn't 'miraculously' fill up when I took a look inside. But there
was a lot more there than I had realised. God was already
answering our prayer of faith. There was enough to keep us
going at least until the end of the week. It might mean eating
some odd things for supper and making some bread rolls instead
of shopping at the baker's. But there was more than enough for
three days of meals.

For the first time in my life I became excited about having
nothing. I realised that when all my resources had gone, I hadn't
even begun to exhaust God's amazing supply. That night I slept
soundly, in the knowledge that God doesn't fail us. I had no idea
what the outcome of that week was going to be, but I had never
felt so certain that God cared for my family and for me.

On Wednesday morning the post arrived at breakfast time as
usual. Among the letters was a brown, unpromising envelope. As
I opened it I could scarcely believe my eyes. It was an anonymous
cheque for £50. 'Praise the Lord!' I said. Barbara agreed. It
looked as if baked beans were off the menu that night after all.
That letter was just the beginning. God bountifully proved to us
beyond all reasonable doubt that he, and not the money supply,
was in control of our welfare.

During the next few weeks leading up to Christmas, all sorts
of doors started to open. By the end of the year we had received,
or been promised in gifts, over £3,500. Even today as I look back
on it, I can hardly believe it all happened. But when we invest
our confidence in God and what he can do, we will look at our
resources completely differently.

Receiving money from other people was a humbling experience. It is much easier to give than to receive. As God 'opened heaven's windows' (see Mal. 3:10) and showered gifts upon us I felt so unworthy to receive this provision of his love. I had no special faith, no great courage, no personal priority line to God's resources. The experience of God's giving us something in abundance reminded me that generosity is part of the very nature of God. Jesus drew attention to this when he drove home his message about money worries:

> Look at the birds: they do not sow seeds, gather a harvest and put it in barns; yet your Father in heaven takes care of them! Aren't you worth much more than birds? Can any of you live a bit longer by worrying about it? (Matt. 6:26–7 TEV).

The last time we went to Scotland I bought some binoculars. I used them to look at the birds and how they behaved. On one occasion, while driving towards Gairloch, we spotted a huge buzzard. It was soaring above the shoreline of Loch Maree – one of the most spectacular places on the West Coast. I pulled into the lay-by, pointed wildly in the air trying to tell the children how important it was, and then focused on the beautiful creature.

Without effort, its huge wings lifted it high into the air. We got the bird book out, tried to identify its markings and then talked about how it survived the hostile weather that was starting to close in around us. 'Look at the birds,' Jesus said. 'Focus upon them for a moment and ask yourself this question: Who feeds them? How do they survive the terrible winters? Where do they get all their supplies from?'

The truth is that no one had to remember to leave food out for the buzzard soaring above us in the Scottish Highlands. It didn't have to earn its living; it simply spent its time looking for what God had already provided. In the same way God provides for us. Do we recognise what he has already provided for us? Do we see God's hand on our daily supply of food and understand that God has remembered us?

Can a mother forget the baby at her breast and have no
compassion on the child she has borne? Though she may
forget, I will not forget you! See, I have engraved you on the
palms of my hands (Isa. 49:15–16).

'Don't worry about money,' Jesus said; we can leave that to God.

Christ helps us to give

On the other side of our garden wall there is a concrete
pavement; it forms part of the churchyard. I walk past it nearly
every day and usually don't notice it. It isn't very attractive, and
part of our development plans for extending the church buildings
includes a proposal to turn this area into a garden. However, the
other day I saw something that made me stop in my tracks. Large
beautiful wild daisies, thirty centimetres tall, were growing
between the cracks in the concrete. No one had planted them;
they just appeared. I suddenly realised that God was way ahead
of us in our development plans!

[Jesus said] And why worry about clothes? Look how the wild
flowers grow: they do not work or make clothes for themselves.
But I tell you that not even King Solomon with all his wealth
had clothes as beautiful as one of these flowers. It is God who
clothes the wild grass – grass that is here today and gone
tomorrow, burnt up in the oven. Won't he be all the more
sure to clothe you? How little faith you have! (Matt. 6:28–30
TEV).

If God can clothe something as unpromising as concrete, how
much more likely is he to be generous in clothing us? It is
because God is so extravagant in supplying our needs that we can
afford to be like this in our giving to other people. We need to
allow him to use what he has given us to help others. The way
we give says more about 'who controls the money supply' in our
homes than anything else.

Soon after we got married Barbara and I decided that before

we spent any of our income, 10 per cent should be set aside for
charitable giving. It was a test of faith to do this because we
could easily justify keeping all of the money for ourselves. We
were newly married and had lots of expenses to be met. We had
no car or home of our own and 10 per cent of our income would
pay for a car and leave us a little left over to start saving for a
mortgage. But we decided we should start our life together as we
meant to go on. Giving a tenth of our income was a small way of
saying to others how good God had been to us.

The important thing here is the attitude of our hearts; it is not
what we give so much as the away we give it that really counts in
God's eyes. That was why Jesus made so much of 'the widow's
mite' (Luke 21:1–4). It is a lot better to give a little gladly, than
to give 5, 10, 15, or 100 per cent grudgingly.

The tithe or tenth was a principle used by the people of God
in the Old Testament. As Christians we are not under law and
should not be pressurised by well-meaning church leaders or
anyone else into a legalistic percentage figure, as though we are
paying God some sort of tax. The Spirit speaking through the
psalmist reminds us that God doesn't need any of our resources
to accomplish his will (though he gladly chooses to use them):

And yet I do not need bulls from your farms or goats from
your flocks; all the animals in the forest are mine and the cattle
on thousands of hills. All the wild birds are mine and all living
things in the fields ... Let the giving of thanks be your
sacrifice to God, and give the Almighty all that you promised
(Ps. 50:9–14 TEV).

Setting aside a certain percentage of our income each month
does not make us somehow better than anyone else. But it
reminds us that God is in control of the money supply and as
God is so generous to us we should copy him. St Paul sums this
up in a spiritual law:

Remember that the person who sows few seeds will have a
small crop; the one who sows many seeds will have a large

crop. Each one should give, then, as he has decided, not with regret or out of a sense of duty; for God loves the one who gives gladly (2 Cor. 9:6–7 TEV).

Let me return to our honeymoon in the Lake District to sum up. At 8.30 on Thursday morning there was a knock at our door. It was the owner calling us to the telephone; someone from the bus depot in Keswick was on the line. The suitcase had been found. It was on its way to Keswick and we could pick it up that afternoon. No new set of clothes after all!

As I put the receiver down, we all had a good laugh about it. What a pity that this was our last day in the Lakes. We never did unravel the mystery behind the lost case: why had it gone missing for so long? Why hadn't it been discovered until Thursday? But God had a purpose in it all. He taught us from the start of our home life together that we could depend on him completely for everything we needed in life. It is a lesson I have had to learn over and over again.

When we arrived home in Gillingham that week there was a pile of wedding presents from family and friends waiting in our flat. As we opened them we were reassured by the generosity of our friends. God used their giving to us to underline this important lesson that he will provide. Every one of the things we needed to turn the flat into our home was provided.

Nothing was duplicated. Nothing was missing. Even the colour schemes people had chosen for things like washing-up bowls and draining racks blended in. It was one of the most amazing experiences of my life. Among the torn-off wrappings and the piles of presents we wept again, this time for joy. We praised God for his faithfulness and asked that all he had given us might be used for him.

And God is able to give you more than you need, so that you will always have all you need for yourselves and more than enough for every good cause. As the scripture says, 'He gives generously to the needy; his kindness last for ever' (2 Cor. 9:8–9 TEV).

Money worries? Yes, we still have them in our home from time to time. But we are learning by God's grace, to leave them with him.

9

QUALITY TIME

Have you ever heard a parent say, 'The thing I most regret is that when my children were young I spent too much time with them'? No, I haven't either. Usually the exact opposite is the case.

Richard's father was a faithful and devoted member of the company. He worked in the city from Monday to Friday and was often away from home at weekends. His job was well paid; his family enjoyed a comfortable standard of living. But his children rarely had much contact with him. Sometimes he was home for supper in the evening, and this gave the family time to 'catch-up' with him. However, mealtime conversations would run something like this:

Son: Have you had a good day at work, Dad?
Dad: Yes. Not bad.
Son: What have you been doing today, Dad?
Dad: Just the usual.
Son: Like what?
Dad: This and that.
Son: What sort of things do you do, Dad?
Dad: Look Son, can we talk about this another time. I'm really tired at the moment.

'Another time' never came. In fact in the whole of his family life, Richard could never remember having a conversation with his father of any length. What a tragedy. Yet the truth is that all too many of our homes can become like this. They become places where we eat, sleep, watch television and occasionally have sex with our partner. There are lots of reasons why this happens. The main one is lack of discipline in the way we use our time.

At a time management course I attended, the speaker gave us a little test to set ourselves. He suggested that the next time we were at our desks working we put a mark on a piece of paper every time we picked it up. It was a good suggestion. Too many marks on something from the 'in' or 'pending' tray meant it was time to put it in the bin.

Then he made another suggestion: never touch a piece of paper more than once. This would make sure we didn't waste any time on things that weren't important. I wonder what would happen if we applied that to our family life.

Try putting a mark on your children's foreheads every time you touch them. I don't mean necessarily a hug or a kiss or a 'hand on head' sort of touch. I mean the sort of touch which actually makes contact with the person: eyeball to eyeball; heart to heart; soul to soul. Ask yourself this: when was the last time I actually made this sort of contact with my son, my daughter or my partner?

Some of us, particularly those of us who work outside the home, need to learn to treat our children and families more like the pieces of paper in our filing trays and our filing trays more like our children and families.

Think about it. We receive a letter; we mull it over; it goes into the pending file. A bit later it comes out again. We read it again. This is a demanding problem – what can be done about it? We pray about it and perhaps we consult some colleagues about it. Meanwhile the letter goes back in the pending slot and gets more and more of our attention. Finally the moment comes to do something with it. We write a response, get our secretary to type it, read what she's written, sign the final draft and then file the original letter away for future correspondence or reference. All this trouble for something which weighs a little more than one of the hairs on our children's heads.

And when we get home, what then? We're tired. It's been a long day. The children have their homework to ask us about: our wife is exhausted by a long day with a terrible toddler and hands him straight over to us. But all our emotional and mental energy has been spent on those letters on the desk.

What would our families be like if we treated them with the same respect and devotion that we give to bits of paper? Of course, our work is important. God has called us to serve him with the whole of our lives and this includes our time in the office, factory, home, or whatever our place of work may happen to be. But he has also called us to live in families. When our job touches us more than our children do, something is wrong. Tomorrow my company may tell me they no longer need my services; I'll be out of a job. But my family will always need me. However old my children are, however long I've been married, my home is 'till death us do part'.

Look back with me at the creation story for a moment. What was God's purpose in creating the universe, the world and all of us in it? Genesis 1 tells us that man did not appear on the scene until the penultimate moment. God was not ready to make human beings until the rest of the world was absolutely perfect. The creation of man and woman was the climax of everything God did:

> Then God said, 'Let us make man in our image, in our likeness, and let them rule over the fish of the sea and the birds of the air, over the livestock, over all the earth, and over all the creatures that move along the ground' (Gen. 1:26).

This suggests to me that people matter more than paper. God was pleased with all of his creation, but human beings touched him in a way nothing else did.

> So God created man in his won image, in the image of God he created him; male and female he created them. God blessed them and said to them, 'Be fruitful and increase in number; fill the earth and subdue it' (Gen. 1:27-8).

God's purpose in all of this was to share himself with us. We see reflections of God's power and glory in the waves thundering on the rocks of a Cornish coastline and in the dancing patterns of gold from an autumn sun dipping gently below the hills. But we see God most of all in other people.

When God came to earth in person, he came as a man and not a towering cedar of Lebanon, or a majestic beast of the field. When Mary held the new-born baby in her arms at Bethlehem, it was God she was holding. When people brought babies to Jesus so that he would bless them it was God who touched them. When the disciples sat down and ate with Jesus it was God who sat opposite them at the table. When the woman who had constant haemorrhaging reached out to Jesus in the crowd, it was God she touched. When the Romans hammered nails into the hands of Jesus, it was God they touched.

Most of us can recognise this truth when our children are born. We see them, their scrunched-up faces and soft pink skin. They are alive and in our arms for the very first time and we think 'Wow! This is incredible.' In those early days we pour out our energy and attention on them without thinking twice about it. They need us to feed them, to clothe them, to wash them, to hold and to comfort them. But somehow as the weeks, months and then years slip by, the novelty of all this wears off.

How would our family life be different if we gave our homes and children the same degree of attention that we did when the baby first arrived? 'You must be joking!' I hear you say. But is it really a joke? What excuse do we give ourselves for treating our toddlers, our primary children, our teenagers or our grown-up children with any less devotion and attention than when they first came into our arms?

I frequently hear comments from parents such as, 'I can't wait until he goes to school; he's driving me mad' or 'Thank goodness the school holidays are nearly over and they'll be out of my hair again' or 'Only a few more years and they'll have left home for good. Bliss.'

Sometimes these things are said in the heat of the moment.

More often they are a true reflection of how we are valuing the time we spend with our kids. How can we avoid the quality of our time at home with them getting lower and lower and lower? Here are some suggestions.

1   Take your parental responsibility seriously

Comments such as the ones we quoted above are understandable in the heat of the moment. But if they reflect our true attitude towards being a parent our families are in trouble.

We feel we have the right to a life of our own, free time, some relaxation and the opportunity to develop our own career. None of these things is wrong intrinsically, but they can easily conflict with how our lives 'touch' those of our children. We may sometimes feel that family life is a drag and get tired of the constant drain on our financial, mental and emotional resources. But we need to remember that children are a gift from God. Every time we diminish their importance in our lives, we are saying something about the value of this gift.

Our responsibility for our children doesn't stop when they go out of the house for school in the morning. They may be no longer 'under our feet' but they are still under our care. This means that we need to find out what they are doing at school so that we can share in it.

There are the obvious opportunities of parents' evenings or school plays. But how about getting involved in the local management of your child's school. Yes, this is time-consuming and can mean piles of paper to read, but it rewards richly. You can find out about the ethos of their school, what the teaching environment is really like and the sorts of struggles your child faces in the school.

We have recently begun getting a prayer group together made up of Christian parents with children at our local schools. This is in its early stages at the moment, but the hope is that it will help to build links with the schools concerned and be a support to the staff.

It may not always be possible to get involved like this. In one of my previous parishes it was virtually impossible to become involved in the local school because of opposition to the church from the head teacher. But all of us can ensure we make time to take an interest in our children's homework. At an early age, this can mean listening to them read at home. When I was a teacher I found that children with parents who listened to them read and took an active interest in the school got on much better than those whose parents didn't seem to bother.

As our children get older, we may find that the homework they are doing is out of our depth. When this happens it may be just the opportunity we need to show them that we can learn something from them! Children can learn a lot from telling us things we didn't know: not least, that we are people who are willing to listen and to learn ourselves – yes, even from people to whom we are normally giving constant advice.

Eventually all our children grow up and will (usually) leave home. This is not the time to say to them or ourselves, 'I've done my bit. Now it's up to you to get on with it.' When children leave home our responsibility for them changes; it doesn't end.

Martin and Laura found this out the hard way. They had marriage problems for years but stuck it out while the children were at home. When the time came for the last one to leave, they decided to abandon their struggle to stay together and began divorce proceedings.

The effect on Sarah, their youngest daughter who had just started university, was traumatic. She was just getting used to being independent and making a life of her own and her parental home represented a secure base which she could come back to at holiday times. The separation left her feeling that her parents had let her down.

This may sound selfish. Parents can't be expected to just 'be there' for their grown-up children whenever they want. Parents, however, can't expect that their behaviour after their children leave home will no longer have an effect on them. It does. Once we become parents we take on a job for life. St Paul, talking about family responsibilities, says this:

> But if anyone does not take care of his relatives, especially the members of his own family, he has denied the faith and is worse than an unbeliever (1 Tim. 5:8 TEV).

The amount of time we need to spend with our children changes as they grow up. But its quality should always say to them 'You matter to me. I love you. To me you're one of the most important people in the world'. The way we treat our children has long-lasting effects on them, on their future home and family, on our society and ultimately on the whole world. We may not be able to give the same level of time and energy to them at twenty as we did at two weeks, but the time we do spend with them should send the same message.

2   Be available on your children's terms

I have found this very difficult. It was easy to grovel around on the floor with them when they were crawling; build bricks with them when they were just learning to co-ordinate movements; hold their hands as we walked together along the pavement and read stories to them on my knee. But as our children have grown up, their terms of reference towards me have changed. They no longer need me to roll around on the floor with them!

At their present stage they need a different sort of attention. For example, they need my attention when I'm eating tea. What happened at school that day may seem 'the most earth-shattering event in human history' and Dad had better listen.

They need my understanding when there's an argument: '"A" is always getting his own way because he's the youngest . . . and he never gets into trouble like I do . . . and he shouldn't have taken back the muscle-man he let me play with . . . so Dad you'd better take my side (or else)'.

They need my compassion when the experience of growing up and hormones drive them mad: 'Why should I have to help with the dishes? I've got piles of homework. Anyway my friends never do anything around the house. You're always going on at me . . .

and Liverpool are playing Everton in five minutes – so (stand clear Mum), I've had enough!'

Giving quality time to our children as they grow up is absolutely exhausting. It's so much easier to say, 'Tell me later' than listen to your son endlessly going on about this 'incredible' computer game he and his mates have invented during lessons. It's much less wearing to tell everyone off and send them all to their bedrooms, than to sit as judge and jury while your children act out the criminal proceedings which led to the dastardly crime. It's tempting to ignore your teenager's tantrums or shout twice as loud as they are, rather than try to pick up the pieces one by one and spend the next half hour in their bedroom talking it through.

Quality time with our children is costly, but bringing Christ into our homes means making the time to be like him:

> Love is patient, love is kind. It does not envy, it does not boast, it is not proud. It is not rude, it is not self-seeking, it is not easily angered, it keeps no record of wrongs. Love does not delight in evil but rejoices with the truth. It always protects, always trusts, always hopes, always perseveres. Love never fails (1 Cor. 13:4–8).

When we allow ourselves time to be touched by our children's excitement, we are helping them to believe that their world matters to us; that we are interested in them; that their words are important to us and are worth taking seriously. When we enter into the real-life conflicts that so often rage in our children's relationships we are helping them to learn about justice, honesty and truth. Our attention to details gives them confidence that help is on its way. When we pour ourselves into our teenagers' traumas, we can help them find the tools to build maturity and a life freed from fear. All this takes quality time and it is exhausting, but it is the example which Christ set us to follow.

Putting this into practice doesn't need to be too much of a big deal. Everyday opportunities arise to 'touch' our children's lives and enter into their world. When their favourite television programme is on, sit down with them and watch it too. When we're out shopping together in the high street, go into the toy department with them and talk to them about the toys they like. Ask them how things work and show an interest in the things that fire their imagination – who knows, it may fire yours too.

When your children have grown up and left home, go to visit them: don't expect them always to come to you. Spend a weekend with them at university, and be ready to let their weird friends come home some time. Meet them for lunch one day when they're at work and let them pay! Make time to get to know your grandchildren: there's no better way of saying to your own children that they still matter and are important in your life. Find the points of contact where you can 'touch' your children's lives, and go for it.

3   Plan your free time together

Most of us live highly pressurised lives. We may have demanding jobs. Both parents in the home may be working. Free time can quickly become a period of convalescence from work rather than recreation.

It became a standing joke in one parish I was in that every time we had a family holiday together I would spend most of it ill. The first day was usually fine; the second there would be a few tell-tale aches and pains; and by Monday morning I would have a throat infection, temperature and grotty headache. On the worst occasion I can remember, Barbara had to call the doctor out. At first he thought I might be having a heart attack! Thankfully it was something quite different, but it made me think that there was something basically wrong with the way we were planning our free time.

Over the years we have struggled with this problem. My job involves working long hours and a six-day week. When holiday times come, there are a lot of things to organise in order to make sure things run smoothly in my absence. This has sometimes turned holidays into a nightmare.

I have finally come to realise that if I want our holiday to be quality time, rather than convalescence time, I have to plan it more carefully. This means making sure, for instance, that I don't work right up until the last minute before we go away. I make sure I have at least one evening free before Friday comes and see that any planning I must do to make the absence possible is sorted out a month beforehand.

As the holiday draws nearer I consciously begin to prepare myself for 'stopping' and don't wait until Saturday morning in a traffic jam on the M25 to start unwinding from work. The discipline of doing all this may sound rather tedious, but it will help to ensure that the Spirit of God can revitalise us rather than having to resuscitate us.

One of the best holidays we ever had was a week after Easter at St Margaret's Bay, just outside Dover. Before we went away we planned what we were going to do each day. This went against the grain for me at first; one of the things I like best about holidays is being free from demands to do things or go to places. However, when you don't plan ahead events can tend to overtake you. If you need a holiday it is probably because you are tired. If you're tired you are not in the best frame of mind to make decisions. Consequently, there is the danger of using up precious holiday time talking about 'What shall we do next?' rather than making the most of the time available.

When we planned ahead what we wanted to do each day we made sure that everyone had a say, there was a good mixture of outings and activities during the week and our finances could be spread out evenly so that when we got home after the holiday we didn't 'feel the draught' in our bank balance. When it came to the holiday itself, we weren't rigid about what we planned to do. If on the day we planned to play tennis it poured with rain, we swapped this with something later in the week.

All of this assumes, of course, that we have the resources to afford a holiday away. There may be times when this just isn't possible. However, in this case it is still possible to plan a week spent 'at home' so as to make it a proper holiday for everyone. For instance you could plan to walk to the local park instead of driving. Or get a video out that everyone can enjoy and have a

Chinese take-away later for Mum and Dad. Go on a ramble in the countryside and make it into a treasure hunt for the children. Have breakfast in bed one day or plan a midnight feast.

We recently had a fascinating 'dream-on' walk through the woods with our four children. We spent the time talking about which career each might follow when they grew up. We imagined one of them becoming a doctor with lots of qualifications; another, an explorer of uncharted territory in far away places; another, a top scientist in demand all over the world; another, a successful journalist with a villa in the Mediterranean where we could all get together for a family holiday once a year. It was only day-dreaming, but tremendous fun.

God has given us the ability to dream and see visions: why not use this gift to enhance our free time? It doesn't cost anything and it will help our children to grow bigger ideas about what God might help them to do. Jesus said, 'If you believe, you will receive whatever you ask for in prayer' (Matt. 21:22). Our free time together takes on a whole new quality when we allow God to set free our imaginations. With him the possibilities are endless.

4   Watch your use of Sundays

I am a traditionalist when it comes to Sundays. I don't like shopping on a Sunday, though I will if we're really desperate. I don't like competitive sport on a Sunday, though a friendly game of football or rounders at the park is good fun.

We have taught our children that Sunday is a special day because it is the day we gather with Christians to worship God. I may be wrong about this old-fashioned approach to the Lord's day. Some people argue that Christians worshipped on the equivalent of our Monday when the church first started (i.e. the first day of the week) so they see no harm in treating Sundays like any other day of the week. Most people I know get a paper on a Sunday, let their children buy sweets or ice creams on a Sunday and see nothing wrong with it. Perhaps when our children are older they will do the same.

My concern is this: does the way we use Sundays today really

represent an improvement on the 'day of rest' idea? Are Sundays
more refreshing now because all traditional sabbath ideas have
been dumped?

I know some of us have to work on a Sunday. I'm one of them.
But the way we use the Lord's day says something about our
attitude to him and the time he has given us. I'm not a killjoy
and don't resent people acting differently to me on Sundays, but
what I see taking place does not look to me like an improvement
on God's pattern of Genesis 2:1–3.

If we treat Sundays just like any other day, then we shall be
tempted to treat God in the same way. What I mean is this:
because the rest of the week we are busy with the everyday
pressures of living, most of us have little chance to stop; think;
pray; seek God's face; wait upon him; or receive from him. The
trouble with treating Sunday like any other day is that the
everyday pressures of life creep in upon us. The issue is not
'Should I buy an ice-cream today?' but 'How can I spend my
time today in a way that shows God matters to me?'

I find that shopping focuses me on the cares of living, however
briefly, and therefore takes my mind off God. Taking part in
competitive sports requires concentration; you cannot focus your
mind on God and on the football or the race track or the road
ahead at the same time. I'm not suggesting we should become
strict sabbatarians and cook Sunday lunch the night before. What
I am saying is that as families we need to ask ourselves how we
use our time on this particular day. The message we send to our
children will be the one they grow up with. Personally I would
like them to grow up always making Sunday special.

Jesus had the most important job to do in the whole of human
history. We will never match his agenda, but we can live by his
principles. He didn't conform to sabbath traditions, but he always
made time to worship in the local synagogue – even if it wasn't
as alive as he might have wished it to be. Jesus had holiday times.
He kept the Jewish festivals, which were the equivalent of our
holy/holidays today. No matter how demanding his schedule, he
made sure that he got quality free time and that those he loved
got it also . . .

It was one of those almost magical times. The disciples had their first chance at putting Jesus's teaching into practice. They'd gone out as he told them to do and ministered to people like he did. To their amazement they found that what he taught them actually worked in practice for them. He'd driven out demons with power and authority: in his name they could do the same. He'd healed sick people and restored them to full health again: in his name they did the same. He'd preached repentance and the forgiveness of sins: in his name they did the same.

As they returned to report back to him, not even the tragic death of John the Baptist could quench their excitement. They were falling over themselves telling him of all that they had seen and done. But Jesus had other things on his mind. He could see the gathering crowds of people; the news of what his disciples had been doing spread like wildfire. There were people in every direction demanding attention. So with great self-discipline and compassionate love, Jesus took the twelve for a boat ride on the lake. 'Come with me,' he said. 'You need to get some rest.' In their great excitement to serve other people, the disciples hadn't even been having proper meals. They had been too busy to bother about their own requirements. But Jesus knew better; he knew they had needs too and he made them stop.

Those few hours with Jesus on the lake felt like a week on the French Riviera. There was something about his presence. Something timeless. Something compelling and wonderful, almost awesome. He let them tell their stories. He listened to them pouring out their souls. And, as they did, he ministered to them (see Mark 6:30–2).

Quality time? Yes, Jesus made sure this was a priority with his friends. Are you doing the same?

10

FAMILY WORSHIP

It's a Sunday morning. The remains of breakfast are being hurriedly scraped into the bin. No chance to wash up; just time to dump the dirties into some soapy water before scrambling into the car for the five-mile journey to church. Meanwhile there's a queue for the bathroom and a riot developing outside the door.

'I'm next,' says a voice.

'No you're not. I was before you!' says another.

'Well, that's too bad. Daddy said I had to go in before you because I need to do my teeth!' comes the reply.

'No he didn't.'

'Yes he did. I'm telling on you. Dad . . .' the voice trails off as I appear on the scene.

'What's going on here? Who's in there?' I ask, banging on the door.

'It's me,' comes the voice of number three. 'I'm on the toilet.'

'Oh no. You're not doing that are you? We'll never get to church on time. Hurry up will you. There are other people out here waiting to come in,' I shout outside the door.

We're supposed to leave by ten o'clock at the latest. It's five past already and still two of the family haven't done their teeth. At last we drag everyone out and pile into the car. Perhaps we'll make up time on the way. The narrow country lanes are thankfully clear. As we speed along to our destination I try to calm down. I tell myself that this scene is being repeated in hundreds of homes across Britain at that moment as families of all shapes and sizes get themselves ready for church.

'We are no different from anyone else,' I say to myself, 'so there's no point getting in a stew about it.' My driving becomes a little more sensible round the narrow bends and I manage to say a few civil words to the people in the back.

Then we arrive. It's a rush to unpack the Sunday school materials and children's clutter in the village hall. No time to help Barbara get things sorted out today; I have to rush back down the hill to the church.

There's the cassette player to set up for recording the sermon; the bread to put out for communion; the flask of hot water to wash up with for later; the various books I need to arrange in my 'pew'; my robes to put on; the hymn numbers to check; the silver on the table to set. Then finally, with moments to spare, I'll go over my sermon notes before the service begins. Then the horrible truth dawns on me: I've left my sermon at home on my desk!

If your experience of worship is anything like mine, bringing Christ into your family's worship is easier said than done. There is a 'Sunday morning conspiracy' which takes place in our home every week. However well prepared we may be, there's always something that happens to make our minds focus on other things.

One of my recurring nightmares is arriving at church without the safe key, or my sermon, or my robes or any of the other hundred and one things I have to remember to bring. This isn't too bad when you live near the church as I do now. But when two of my churches were five and three miles away, forgetting something was no joke.

Your Sunday morning 'nightmare' might be quite different. Maybe for you it's the experience of sitting through a service with two noisy toddlers, or remembering half-way through the first hymn that you've forgotten to put the chicken in, or the sudden realisation that the awkward silence after the third hymn is because your toddler has just made his way into the pulpit and is emptying the contents of the preacher's glass down the steps.

Family worship is a lot more than just what happens in church on a Sunday. In fact, this is a very small part of it. Sundays are not the most important part of family worship at all. The most important worship we experience as families is what goes on from Mondays to Saturdays in our homes. We'll come back to Sunday services in a moment. But first let's look at how to bring worship into the everyday.

Everyday prayers

I used to find talking to God in 'everyday' language impossible. My experience of prayer as a child was through Sunday services. Sunday worship taught me that prayer was something we do in a special building, with a special tone of voice, using special words.

Therefore, whenever I wanted to pray I had a problem. Although I could say the Lord's Prayer and other 'set' prayers, or prayers out of books, I couldn't pray with ordinary, natural words. This caused problems because the prayers I used were very general sorts of prayer. They made God seem very remote and distant to me.

I had learnt that 'Our Father' is 'in heaven' but hadn't come to understand how he can also be present in a real and tangible way. When I first heard of people praying using ordinary language I honestly thought this was blasphemy! How could a mere mortal speak directly to someone like God who is all powerful, perfect, holy, beyond understanding, awesome, majestic, even (at times) terrible in his power? The very idea of 'open' or extempore prayer, was therefore ridiculous and even mad in my view.

When I was a student at teacher training college I found out that some Christians met in each other's rooms to pray, using everyday words. I thought they were weird and decided to steer clear of them. However I became increasingly depressed about my prayer life. Compared to the close and intimate sort of prayer life which these other students seemed to have, I felt very second-rate. It made me think that because I couldn't pray like they could perhaps I wasn't a Christian at all. The breakthrough in my prayer life came one Sunday afternoon. It was a 'safe' day to pray and I was in a 'safe' place to pray – the college chapel. As one of a small group of students gathered together in that building I opened my mouth and spoke.

I don't remember what the prayer was. It was short, uncomplicated and very everyday. For the first time in my life I spoke to God as if he were sitting next to me rather than just out of reach beyond the church roof. This experience changed my Christian life out of all recognition. I began to speak to God about things I'd never dared before.

What most amazed me was the idea that prayer actually worked. I could believe the bit about the 'daily bread' in the Lord's Prayer; it was more difficult to believe that I could pray about the weather, my work, my money troubles, holidays, health, people in other countries and of course my own family.

Don't worry about anything, but in all your prayers ask God for what you need, always asking him with a thankful heart (Phil. 4:6 TEV).

I also realised looking back on my prayer life, that my praying was really a time of 'worrying' rather than asking. Before this I would pray about things but could never trust God to do anything about what was on my mind. Prayers were a way of airing my troubles to God, rather than allowing him to come into them.

This experience of everyday praying has taught me an important lesson. Prayer is the key to having a vitally alive relationship to God in our homes. There are many good books on the market about prayer. But the best one I have ever read came from a second-hand bookstall and cost me 10p. It is O. Hallesby's classic, called simply *Prayer*. Listen to what he says about everyday praying:

To pray is nothing more than to open the door, giving Jesus access to our needs and permitting Him to exercise His own power in dealing with them. He who gave us the privilege of prayer knows us very well. He knows our frame; He remembers that we are dust. That is why He designed prayer in such a way that the most impotent can make use of it. For to pray is to open the door to Jesus, and that requires no strength; it is only a question of our wills. Will we give Jesus access to our needs? That is the one great fundamental question in connection with prayer ... Let us think of patients who are ill with tuberculosis. The physicians put them out in the sunlight and fresh air, both in summer and in winter. There they lie until a cure is gradually effected by the rays of the sun. The recovery of these patients is not dependent upon their thinking, in the sense of understanding the effect of the sun's rays or how these rays work. Neither does their recovery depend upon the feelings they experience during the rest cure. Nor does it depend upon their wills in the sense of exerting themselves to will to become well. On the contrary, the treatment is most successful if the patients lie very quietly and are passive, exerting neither their intellects nor their wills. It is the sun which effects the cure. All the patients need to do is to be in the sun. Prayer is just as simple.

'To pray is to open the door to Jesus.' This simple but profound statement about prayer tells us everything. It is this sort of prayer principle that is at the heart of all good family worship in our home. To pray together in our families is to let Jesus into our lives. It allows him access. It says to him, 'Come in Lord, we need you.' This can be done in the simplest of ways.

If you are not used to praying together as a family, then start saying a 'Thank you for our food' prayer at meal-times. If it embarrasses you to say an 'everyday' prayer you have made up like 'Thank you for our dinner, Lord', try using one of the thank you prayers in books. Your local Christian bookshop will have a good supply of these and this 'set' prayer may help to get you started.

However, don't leave it at this. When you have got used to this idea as a family, try to say one that is 'made up'. You can overcome your feelings or strangeness about this by writing the prayer out beforehand. The more you do this, the more 'natural' it will become to bring Christ into your home at meal-times.

Meal-times are the most important part of the day in my family. They are often chaotic because all the children want to speak at the same time. So we sometimes have to make them speak in turns. The meal table is a place where we can gather together the fragments of the day and make something of them.

There is something very special about these times and we need to guard them as 'family worship' opportunities. Starting a meal with the name of Jesus reminds all of us where food and everyday things come from. Talking about the day as the meal progresses reminds us that all of our lives matter. Sometimes, if there has been a special problem from the day, we will pray about it after we've eaten. This doesn't always happen, but as Jesus is brought into our discussions around the table he can prompt us to turn a care into a prayer. Let me tell you of two memorable occasions when this happened – one at breakfast and one after the evening meal.

We don't often have the chance to eat breakfast all together. Usually our eldest son has left for school before anyone else sits down to eat. So on this occasion there were just the five of us. As usual after we've eaten, one of our children had read a Bible story from a children's 'everyday Bible stories' book. Then we talked about what we could pray for (this was one of the rare days when there was time for this).

Elliott asked if we could pray for his friend Michael who'd been away from school for a while. He was a good companion to Elliott. They walked to school together and this made life easier when he faced a difficult day. When the time came for us to pray I said: 'Lord, please make Michael better so he can come back to school today.' We said 'Amen' and at that very moment the doorbell rang.

Elliott went to open it. It was Michael! As they came in the room together I said to Michael, 'Did you know you're an answer to prayer, Michael? We've just been praying for you to get better and just when we said "Amen" you rang the doorbell!' It was a good story, and it made us all laugh.

Of course family prayers don't always go like this. There are days when we only manage an 'I'll say a prayer for everyone' sort of prayer, or times when the children read a prayer from a children's prayer book, or times when there's been a bad atmosphere and no one wants to pray. But praying together at meal-times has helped the children and even their friends to see what can happen when we bring Christ into our everyday lives.

On another occasion I had an important lesson to learn from my eldest son. It was supper-time and we were talking with the children about plans to buy a house. We have always tried to tell them things that concern us. Sometimes we have to be careful about this; our children need to be protected from getting into 'adult' concerns at too young an age. But buying a house was something that affected them as well as Barbara and me. We'd been looking at possible places and the children had been fully involved in the searching process.

Since Barbara had been working full time, it had become possible to consider a mortgage. For a variety of reasons the time to buy seemed ripe. However, as we talked to our children I shared with them, in simple terms, my concern about the costs of a deposit and all the fees.

We had found the perfect place; Camelot was big enough to use for holidays and near enough to escape to on days off. But raising the finances seemed a huge obstacle. As the meal concluded, I told the children not to get too excited about the idea, just in case we found in the end that we couldn't afford it. It was then that Nathaniel put me in my place. As we were clearing the table he said to me in an exasperated tone, 'Dad, if you need the money, why don't you ask Jesus for it!'

His question stopped me in my tracks. We had been talking all tea-time about the house and yet not once had I suggested praying about it, bringing Christ into the situation. That comment by my son made me feel very small. It reminded me that in all my attempts to train my children to follow Christ and put him first in their lives, I sometimes needed to learn from them.

We stopped what we were doing, took Nathaniel's suggestion and prayed. I'm rather glad we did. The next day a cheque came in the post. It was completely unexpected but had the fingerprints of God all over it. The sum of money isn't important, but it represented exactly half of what we needed for the deposit on the house. Our family worshipped God that day with heartfelt thanks. He had given his answer to our prayer quite dramatically. But more importantly, he had shown us how much we need to be involved in praying together.

There are many ways that we can introduce everyday prayer into family life. Some of the suggestions I have made above may not be practical for your home. Perhaps you don't eat meals together, or when you do it is too difficult to make this discipline work. If this is the case, try starting prayers together at another regular time, such as bedtime. When our children are very tiny this may be a lot more practical than struggling for a few moments peace with junior screaming to get out of the high chair. The emphasis needs to be on 'everyday' because unless prayer in our homes and families is 'everyday' our children will grow up without seeing how real and natural prayer can be.

Signposts to God

It was a day that would live for ever in their minds. God had safely brought the people of Israel into the promised land. It had taken forty years of diversions, set-backs, disappointments, failures and many deaths. But at last the day came when God called the people to cross over.

The Jordan at that time of year was in flood. This made it both dangerous and impractical to cross. Imagine wading through unknown flood waters with babies and children, animals and other livestock – not to mention the worldly possessions that the Hebrews had carried with them. Most of them were loaded; the Egyptians had been so desperate to get rid of them in the end that they almost paid them to leave with gold, silver and fine clothes (see Exod. 12:33–6).

Although most of the original exiles from Egypt were now dead, their families had inherited the treasures. These would be lost in the flood waters or else left behind on the shores for other passers-by to receive. They could have walked down-river until a possible crossing place could be found, but there was no guarantee of this and in travelling they were bound to come across some of the old enemies that they'd left behind on their travels.

Then it happened. To prove to them he was faithful, God called Joshua to send the Ark of the Covenant into the flood waters first. This was almost unthinkable. The ark represented the most precious thing in the whole of Israel. It was the covenant box where the ten commandments were sealed. It symbolised the very presence of God himself among his people. To risk losing it meant losing everything that mattered most to God's people: his law, his special treaty with them and his divine presence.

The priests led the way ahead into the raging water. There was something almost final about the moment; it was as if the fate of God's people rested upon the next few seconds. Humanly speaking the journey was over: as the ark disappeared into the murky waters, everyone else would follow suit and that would be the last anyone saw of a 'promised land' again. This was like D-Day for the people of God.

Everyone held their breath as those in front of the ark reached the edge of the flood. They didn't stop. Joshua had promised them all would be well. And it was. As they moved forward the water began moving away from them. The flood was receding.

Moments later there was dry ground in front of the Hebrew nation, where once there had been fatal floods. People living downstream wondered what on earth had happened. Those upstream got more water than they'd ever seen before as the flood water began mysteriously pouring into the region of Zarethan. There were thousands of people gathered together to cross on that day, and not one of them got wet (Josh. 3).

No one in Israel could remember a day like it except Joshua, who had seen God do something similar to the Red Sea forty

years earlier. It was a not-to-be-forgotten day. This was a story
to tell to your children around the campfire, for them to pass on
to their children and so on down through all generations. And to
make sure that the incredible event wasn't forgotten, Joshua told
the twelve leaders of the nation each to get a stone from the
middle of the river. They brought them to him on the west bank,
and at a place called Gilgal Joshua built a monument from them.

> He said to the people of Israel, 'In the future, when your
> children ask you what these stones mean, you will tell them
> about the time when Israel crossed the Jordan on dry ground.
> Tell them that the LORD your God dried up the water of the
> Jordan for you until you had crossed, just as he dried up the
> Red Sea for us. Because of this everyone on earth will know
> how great the LORD's power is, and you will honour the LORD
> your God for ever' (Josh. 4:21–4 TEV).

Did Joshua's idea work? Judge for yourself. You can read the
whole story in the Bible today. It shows us how valuable it is in
our families to do things that help us to remember what God has
done.

This idea of a monument or marker is a marvellous way of
bringing family worship alive in our homes today. You and I may
not be expert stone masons, but all of us have access to a camera
even if it's only a throw-away one. The camera enables us to do
what Joshua did on the shores of the Jordan River: to erect a
faith 'signpost' so that whenever we look at the photo album and
ask 'What were these pictures about?' we can tell the story of
what God has done.

Let me give a practical example of this. In 1981 Barbara and I
began praying with the children about our next move. We
couldn't tell them all the details; we simply told them that God
had the right place for us to go and if we asked him to show us
the way, he would. Early in April that year, we responded to a
letter from the Bishop of Carlisle which invited us to consider a
parish in Cumbria. It was a rather out-of-the-blue suggestion

and wasn't exactly close to London where we were living at the time.

However, for a number of reasons we felt that this might be the place God was calling us to go to next. We arranged to see the parish and, one Saturday, left on the 6.15a.m. train from Euston. We took one of our children with us so we could use a family railcard ticket, but left the other three at home.

In order to keep a record of this journey and explain to the children where we'd been, I took my camera. I used it on the train to record the journey. I took pictures out the window – the Heinz factory in North London, the countryside whizzing past us as we sped north, then finally the cosy armchair figures of the Howgill Fells. When we got off the train at Penrith we even stopped on the platform for a photo. As the Team Rector gave us a grand tour of the 120-sq-mile parish in his tiny grey Peugot 205, I snapped away at everything we saw.

It was an exhausting trip to do in a day. But when we arrived home late on Saturday night, my camera contained all we needed in order to show the children where we had been and where God might want us to go.

Some weeks later, having decided to make the move, we went back. This time Barbara and I drove up on our own. We took more photographs and even went inside the bungalow we were to live in temporarily and took lots of photos. By the time we'd finished toing and froing we had collected a full pictorial record of God's call to us to one of the most beautiful places on earth.

The pictures helped us to remember what we had seen and where we were going. But they were more important than that. They helped us look back later on when things got tough in the Lake District and say, 'What do these pictures mean? They tell us that we are in this place because Almighty God brought us here. This is no accident, this is "his-story" and we're where God wants us to be for now'.

Photographs are only one method that we can use to 'signpost' the activity of God in our family life. It may be that you think of other things. Some people collect souvenirs on holiday: keeping an album of these helps to remind themselves, 'Yes, that was the place such and such happened. Wasn't that a great family time? God really blessed us in that place, didn't he.'

Other people, who can afford them or inherit them, like antiques. These can be a reminder of places you've lived or people who've loved you and given things to you. These sit in our homes as silent signposts reminding us of what God has done: they record encounters we have had with a faithful, wonderful God who is ever present and ever ready to reveal himself to us in the everyday.

Documenting God's goodness to us can also be a great help. I have started keeping a special place in my filing cabinet marked 'encouragements'. I put in it letters, and other written evidence of God's activity and faithfulness in our family's life. For instance, I once had a letter from the Archbishop's administrative assistant. It came as quite a surprise to get a letter with 'Lambeth Palace' stamped on it.

Apparently the family of someone I had conducted a funeral for were so grateful for my ministry that they wrote to Archbishop Robert Runcie about it! I was really encouraged by this letter, shared it with my family and decided to file it as a tribute to the goodness of God in our lives. It was as if God was saying to me, 'What you are doing is valuable to me, and don't you ever forget it.' Family life needs lots of encouragement, and when I get a letter like this (let me say it's the only one from this particular source) I find myself worshipping the God who has called someone as sinful as me to be of use to him.

What reminders do you have in your home that point you to the greatness and goodness of God? Are there any? Wouldn't it be a good idea to invest in a few? Signposts of God's faithfulness in our homes inspire a family to worship him.

Family worship is about a heart-attitude to God in our homes, not about what we do on a Sunday. When we meet with God in everyday life and know we have done it, then the natural response of our hearts will be to praise him for all he has done. There are so many negative things to bring our family lives down into the doldrums. Working at our everyday worship together pays great dividends and leaves a mark on the world where God has been.

Children in church

I have great sympathy with parents who find bringing children to church a real struggle. It is! I have experienced a whole variety of different sorts of worship during the course of ministry. Family services I've been to have ranged from chaos with visual aids, to 1662 sung matins with line drawings from the pulpit.

In one church which we attended, the services were all from the Book of Common Prayer. There was no Sunday school, no modern music, no crèche, no family-friendly anything. My memories of those days of trying to keep a toddler and new baby quiet during this 'trip back to a lost era' are not happy ones. Fortunately many churches today do everything possible to include children.

For some congregations, all-age family worship is now the norm; children are involved in worship every Sunday and great efforts are made to be family-friendly. This is great progress on 1662 with pictures. I recently asked our children to tell me what church activities helped them most in their worship of God. Here are their top ten:

1 Lively worship.

2 Dad's sermons. (*Amazing! I promise you this wasn't prompted by me.*)

3 All-age family services.

4 Special services at Christmas and Easter.

5 Sunday groups like Pathfinders, CYFA and Sunday school/ club.

6 Church picnics and game days.

7 Church house parties away from home.

8 Belonging to Brownies. (*Encouraging to hear. Our uniformed organisations can be a real 'God-send' to our young people when they are Christ-centred.*)

9 Celebrations. (*E.g. a 'Light Party' at Halloween; a 'Christmas Crackers' service on Christmas Eve.*)

10 Special youth and children's services.

I am in favour of anything we can do as a church to help family worship on a Sunday to be relevant, alive and life-changing. In my present parish we are constantly reviewing what we do with children and young people and asking 'Can we do better?' This is all part of fulfilling the scriptural principle in Deuteronomy 4:9–10:

> Be on your guard! Make certain that you do not forget, as long as you live, what you have seen with your own eyes. Tell your children and your grandchildren about the day you stood in the presence of the LORD your God at Mount Sinai, when he said to me, 'Assemble the people. I want them to hear what I have to say, so that they will learn to obey me as long as they live and so that they will teach their children to do the same' (TEV).

And Jesus's concern for children in Matthew 19:14 and Mark 10:14:

> Jesus said, 'Let the children come to me and do not stop them, because the Kingdom of heaven belongs to such as these' (TEV).

Growing spiritual pains

Let me tell you about Ginny. I met her at 'Play Group'. This was a play scheme I ran when I was a student at teacher training college. The project was for young people who lived in the local community around the campus. We met them each Saturday afternoon and ran a varied programme of activities for about two hours. All ages of children came along, from one to fifteen years old; no one was turned away. I first came across Ginny when she was eleven. She had straight jet-black hair, eyes that flashed like steel and a temper which dared you to cross her. She was thin, wiry, smoked like a trooper and most of the other children were scared of her (with good reason).

Ginny was my first true introduction to youth work; she gave me a hard time. Like most of the children who came to the play project, Ginny was from a deprived background. She tested the limits of our patience every week and it was tempting to ban her – especially when she once helped to wreck a hall we had been meeting in. But as I got to know her the real challenge for me was a personal struggle of faith. As a committed Christian leader (the project itself was non-sectarian) I wondered how I could bring Christ into my friendship with children like Ginny who normally would never have gone near a church (except to vandalise it) and for whom the name of Christ was only a swear word.

The breakthrough came one autumn. It happened in a way I'd least expected. It was the first term of my second year at college. By now I had established a friendship with Ginny and some of the other children. I persuaded them to take part in a Christmas drama production in the college chapel at the end of term. This had the full support of the other students involved in the project, and was welcomed cautiously by the college authorities (they too had heard of Ginny's reputation). I shall never forget the first practice we had in the chapel. The sight of twenty-five tear-aways climbing all over the church furniture, playing hide and seek behind the communion table, and using the main aisle as a skid track had to be seen to be believed. After the first five minutes of complete chaos I could not imagine how I had got myself into this. By the end of the first practice I was ready to give up. Each week I told myself that they would respond better next time. The day came for the dress rehearsal; it was a shambles. Those young people with speaking parts hadn't learned their lines properly and the rest of them were out of control. By now the invitations had gone out and the children were all expecting their tea party 'treat' afterwards. I left the chapel that afternoon with a very heavy heart. My attempts to introduce these children to something explicitly Christian had failed.

The production was scheduled to take place the next day. When I woke up that morning I knew there was nothing I could do but place the children into God's hands. I had done all that I could; the rest was now up to him. Despite the memory of the dress rehearsal I found myself feeling a deep sense of peace as I made my way to the chapel after lunch. I had no idea what was going to happen; I couldn't even be certain that the children would turn up. All I had was the assurance in my heart that if everything went wrong then at least we had tried. But that afternoon I was in for a surprise. All the children turned up in good time, they co-operated all through the final preparations and when it came to the production itself they shone like stars! The music was cued, the cast mobilised and the two leading figures made their way down the long stately central aisle to the strains of Neil Diamond's 'Dear Father ... we dream' (from *Jonathan Livingstone Seagull*). And it really did feel like a dream! All the nightmare rehearsals, the threatened cancellations and the risk of failure had given way to one of the most moving nativities I have ever seen ... with Ginny in the central role as Mary. 'Only Jesus could achieve this,' I thought, as with a lump in my throat I watched Ginny make her way to 'Bethlehem' at the front of the chapel, leaning on the arm of Garry who was six inches shorter. It was a moment to savour. The children, including Ginny, rose to the occasion and performed perfectly. The drama had been a leap of faith on my part, but it had paid off.

This event taught me a vital lesson about bringing Christ to young people. The greatest spiritual struggle is sometimes not with them but with ourselves. We can and should do all we can to make Jesus's life and teaching real to them, but in the end we need to leave the outcome with him. This is what I think the writer of Proverbs was getting at when he said 'Train up a child in the way that he should go and when he is old he will not depart from it' (22:6). God is far more interested in the direction our children are heading than in the route they take to get there.

When Ginny and the other children came out of the chapel it took them less than five minutes to revert to anarchy. But the point is that we had directed them to Jesus for a few hours of their chaotic lives. We should never underestimate the long-term effect that this can have.

The challenge of spiritual 'boredom'

I once heard a well-known disc jockey say that Christianity offered one of the dullest experiences around. To look at the faces of some of our young people in church on a Sunday morning, I am inclined to agree with him. They are bored with the singing, bored with the standing up and sitting down, bored with the 'Cook's tour of the world' type prayers, and definitely bored with my sermon. Spiritual boredom is a common disease which most teenagers get at some time or other as they grow up. Is there a cure?

I know this is a particularly difficult area for those of us with older teenagers in our family or church. As parents we may have nutured them in the faith from the moment they were born, seen them through Sunday school (or the equivalent), watched them begin to take an active part in the life of the church and then just as we think they are going to stay the course the rumblings begin. 'Why should I go to church? It's boring. None of my friends go.' – 'The church is full of hypocrites.' – 'Only old people go to church: they're a load of "fuddy-duddies"' – 'You don't have to go to church to be a Christian.' – 'No way am I ever going to be confirmed!' These are the sort of things young people think and say.

We're going through a period of this sort of 'rumbling' in our church family at the moment. We have a balcony and each week most of the teenagers sit in one corner of it (my eldest son being one of them). Some of them talk all the way through the service; they make rude comments about what's going on down at the front; most of them don't sing; they think the sermons are one big yawn; they are there under sufferance. The problem came to a head recently. My wife Barbara was chatting after the service with a fairly new member of the church. In the course of conversation the subject of the young people's behaviour that morning arose. The new person was surprised to learn that all the teenagers concerned were from Christian backgrounds: she had presumed that the reason they behaved so badly was that they all came from non-church backgrounds and hadn't got used to sitting in services yet. Oh heartache!

How do we handle this sort of disaffection among our teenagers? It is a common problem in Britain today. Peter Brierley has produced some excellent research into teenagers and the church based on the English Church Census in 1989. In his book *Reaching and Keeping Teenagers* he writes:

> In 1979 13 per cent of England's teenagers attended church. Ten years later the proportion had fallen to 9 per cent … This was a decline from 490,000 15–19-year-olds to 345,000. But the drop for all teenagers (those aged 10–19) is even greater. Estimating the numbers in church for every ten-year age group in 1979 compared with the 1989 figures … reveals a decline of nearly half in the number of teenagers attending.[2]

These figures are startling. They tell us that on average, 300 teenagers a week are leaving the church! This is bad news. What can we do about it? We could:

1 Do nothing
Some of us are so punch-drunk by statistics that we assume they cannot be changed. We see the trend in teenage disaffection as inevitable. We resign ourselves to the conclusion that nothing can be done.

2 Blame ourselves
Some of us look at the problem and see it as a personal failure. We sympathise with the attitude of young people to the church. We see no way out of the problem and feel guilt-ridden every time one of our teenagers becomes just another statistic.

3 Blame other people

This is a popular way out. The minister or other leaders in our church are blamed for being out of touch with the teenage culture, having no idea how to get them involved and expecting them to conform to what the adults do. Other members of the congregation are blamed for having unrealistic expectations about the ways young people should behave and contribute to the life of the church. This makes the teenagers feel more and more isolated until eventually they vote with their feet.

4 Wait and see

Others of us may be very sceptical about surveys and statistics. We don't take the figures too seriously and prefer to wait and see what happens in the next few years. 'After all,' we say to ourselves, 'everyone knows you can prove anything with statistics.'

I have now worked among young people for over twenty years and during this time I have found all these approaches tempting to follow myself, but I am not happy with any of them. Although they each contain a grain of truth, they all produce a rather negative approach to spiritual growing pains in young people. I am convinced that there is a better way. Here are some guidelines which I have found can help us to support and reach young people as they struggle to grow up into the Christian faith.

1 Communicate with them

Communication is something which needs to be constantly worked at. One mother put it to me like this: 'My teenage son doesn't talk any more; he grunts. I can't get a civil word out of him at the meal table.' She told me how she dealt with this on one occasion. During one particular meal-time she became increasingly frustrated by her son's behaviour. Every time she asked him a question the best reply he could manage was a grunt. Eventually she decided to respond to him in his own cave-man-type language: scooping up some mashed potato, she flicked a spoonful of it straight at him. The strategy scored a direct hit! Her son was so surprised at what she did that he just sat there open-mouthed in astonishment. At last she had his undivided attention. Over the washing-up the family all had a good laugh about what had happened; more seriously they were able to talk about the lack of verbal communication that had become part of their family life. What an example of communication.

I am not suggesting that we should use shock tactics like these to make our teenagers talk to us. But sometimes it is worth showing them we are serious about getting through. Barbara recently tried a different sort of idea out on our 'balcony teenagers'. She hasn't got specific responsibility for this age group in the church at the moment, but used to teach this present group of teenagers when they were in the Pathfinders (11–13s). While doing the ironing one Sunday evening she had an idea. She decided to get these young people together. Each of them was sent a 'mysterious' invitation to come to our home for 'A Chat, some Coke, some Crisps, some mystery prizes and the fourth 'C'' (which wasn't explained but stood for Christ). They all turned up, curious about why they had been invited. Most of them had guessed about the fourth 'C', but they listened to what she had to say about their attitude to Christ on Sunday mornings (she has first-hand experience of what they get up to in the balcony because she sits right in front of them on a Sunday). They in turn told her frankly what they thought of the church services and the church family. In less than forty minutes they had covered topics ranging from being allowed to say rude things in a service, to putting half-chewed sweets in the collection bag as it was passed round. It was great communication and a lot of positive things came out of it.

2 *Take an interest in them*

One of the things our young people complained about in their meeting with Barbara was their belief that the church family weren't really interested in them. They felt devalued. I found this very surprising when Barbara told me about it afterwards. We have done everything possible to include them. We give them responsibility in Sunday Club activities which take place on a Sunday morning; we encourage them to take part in reading lessons and act as sidespeople; they arrange, plan and lead a service themselves regularly ... In fact I sometimes think we try too hard to accommodate them: and this is precisely the point! They are not miniature adults, but adolescents. There is no harm in getting them to do adult things in the church or in our own homes, but we must never forget that they are people in their own right. We need to allow them to make their own special contribution to our homes and churches. This means taking trouble to find out precisely what this is.

In their excellent book *The Brat Pack*, John and Sue Ritter put it like this:

Next Sunday, when you go to your service, have a look around you and put yourself in the position of your young people. Don't kid yourself, look properly with an open mind. I'll tell you what you'll see. You'll see kids who don't mind coming up the front and reading the Bible, kids who will even get up and do some kind of drama ... but you won't find many kids *singing*! When 'worship time' comes around, it's time to find the jacket fluff. Yes, I know you enjoy it, but your kids don't! No, they don't! It's a fact, kids don't sing any more. They don't sing in assembly, they don't sing in music lessons ... they don't sing![3]

This doesn't mean that we should stop singing hymns or worship songs just in order to fit in with them. It means we need to find a way of helping them to get involved and stay involved in the religious experience we call 'Church'.

With this in mind I recently tried an experiment. Each year the local secondary school come to church for their carol service. It is a great privilege to have this link with them. However I find it one of the most challenging things I have to do all year. The order of service, the carols ... everything is left up to me to organise. Choosing carols that they will know (and be prepared to sing) is very hard indeed. So in December 1994 I took a risk; I omitted one of the carols we usually sing and put in a rap instead. I used the words of 'Away in a manger', concluding that if I could get them to respond to a rap based on a carol like this (which was usually sung by small children half their age) I could get away with anything.

To my amazement it worked. The young people were captivated by it and later the Head Teacher told me they were rapping 'Away in manger' around the school for the rest of the day. 'Praise God!' I thought: here was something that we could use in church to show young people that Christianity was on their wavelength. I used the same idea at several other Christmas services that year and each time I had a great response from young people.

Take time to find out what your teenagers are interested in, and then be prepared to take a few risks. In my experience, if this is done prayerfully it always reaches the target.

3 *Get real*

One of the latest catch-phrases used by teenagers is 'Get a life'. I'm not sure who started it but it could well be applied to our attitude to adolescents. Young people see through sham and hypocrisy very quickly indeed. For instance, one of the things our teenagers say when we complain about them talking through the services is – 'What about the grown-ups? They do it: why shouldn't we?' They have a point. We need to be sure that as Christians, whether on Sunday mornings in church services or on Monday mornings fighting to get a space in the bathroom, we practise what we preach. Adult hypocrisy seriously damages the health of young people's faith.

Many teenagers leave church because they look at what their parents are like or other adult Christians and think to themselves 'If that's what being a Christian is, then count me out.' They watch how we treat them; they notice when (or if) we pray and read our Bibles; they take note of the way we treat our partner; they pick up our attitude to the Minister and other members of the church, especially those we don't like very much. They watch how we live day by day and ask themselves 'Is Jesus real to these people? Does he make a difference in Mum and Dad's life? Is he someone worth giving up sleep for on a Sunday morning?' I find this a constant challenge in my life. We may be able to fool our Christian friends, our Minister and even some of our relatives that our Christian life is consistent and 'together', but we can't fool kids. They can see right through us. The best way to win their trust and respect is to be ready to admit our failures, ask their forgiveness when we are in the wrong and be prepared to show them that we struggle at being a follower of Jesus sometimes too.

In my own family and local church the jury is still out on the verdict; I am not sure whether we have done enough to help our teenagers survive their spiritual struggles. In this sense we are in a 'wait and see' situation. However I am convinced that 'he who began a good work' in their lives will be faithful to complete it (Phil. 1:6); or as the Psalmist wrote:

'My soul, wait thou only upon God; for my expectation is from him.' (Ps. 62:5 AV)

The right balance

All this does not mean that we should worship the family. There is a delicate balance to strike here. The family is God's basic unit and building-block for community living in our world. It is only right that it should play a dominant part in the pattern of worship on a Sunday. We should not need to apologise for 'Happy-clappy' music or 'Childish visual aids'. Those who make comments like these about family worship need to search their hearts to see if the child God has called them to be is still alive in there somewhere (see Matt. 18:3).

However, those of us concerned for children and families in church need to be reminded sometimes that true family worship is about valuing Christ above all. When children and families become the main motivation for our service planning, sermon writing and money spending in church, we need to ask ourselves why we are in church on a Sunday. Christ must always be raised above all.

In practice, this means that those of us attending churches which are family-friendly need to ask whether the single people, widows and other 'marginal' groups in the church family are being hindered or helped by our Sunday service. Those of us in churches that aren't family-friendly need to ask ourselves whether we should be doing something to change this.

It may be that God will use you and your family to start something new in your church. There are plenty of excellent resources to help start Sunday schools or improve family services. With love and patience you may enable your local church to discover that family worship brings the worship of Christ alive to all ages, not just children. For all of us, the challenge of worship is all-consuming and all-demanding. Jesus said:

'Love the Lord your God with *all* your heart and with *all* your soul and with *all* your mind and with *all* your strength' (Mark 12:30).

This means having an everyday attitude to worship that spills over from Sundays into all the other days of our week.

11

SEPARATION

This is one chapter I would rather leave out. Maybe that's why I've left it to nearly the end of the book. But it is an important chapter because it deals with an issue that every family has to face at some time.

When I was five years old my mother had to go into hospital. There were four children in the family at that stage. My brother was three and my two elder sisters were nine and seven. As the treatment in hospital was going to take a number of weeks, my parents decided to send us to stay with relatives. I found this an awful idea. We lived in the Lake District at the time and our nearest relatives were 260 miles away in Bristol. There was no M6 in those days, only mile upon mile of long distance travelling.

To be in Bristol when my parents were at the other end of the country just felt terrible. All of us were homesick, but I was definitely the worst! My grandmother and aunt looked after me very well, but I was so upset that in the end my father had to come and get me. Leaving the others behind, I was taken back to Barrow-in-Furness and somehow Dad managed to take care of me while Mum continued her treatment in hospital.

Thirty-three years later I'm afraid there hasn't been much improvement in my response to family separations. During the autumn of 1994 my period of study leave meant being separated from Barbara and the children from Sunday to Friday night. We spent the weekends together, but the rest of the time I was on my own. At first I thought I should be fine. I'd been away on mid-week conferences before and managed to cope all right.

This was different. It was the second Sunday of my sabbatical and we'd all sat down for tea. We have a Sunday tradition in our family; at teatime Dad serves up freshly-made scones, hot from the oven. We began this tradition years ago when we'd run out of bread one Sunday. It had gone down so well with the children that it became a regular weekly routine.

This week Elizabeth had helped me with the cooking and everyone was looking forward to tucking in to the steaming plateful of lovely food. Suddenly it was as if someone had turned on a tap behind my eyes. Without warning and without being able to stop, my eyes filled up and tears began rolling down my cheeks. The children didn't know what to think. This had never happened to me before, and they all wondered what was the matter. When I told them why I was so upset, they were all soon following suit and before long the tissue box was nearing empty.

It was weeks before I adjusted to this enforced separation. At one point I had to abandon the struggle and return home. It wasn't an easy time in our family; it put pressure on all our relationships. But I'm very glad I went through it because the experience taught me to value family life a little better. I now understand more clearly what separation can mean. Let's look at three possible causes of separation and see how bringing Christ into the situation can help us through.

1 Deliberate choice

Some of the separation we experience in our family life can come through deliberate choice. One year Barbara and I decided to go skiing. The cost for all of us to go was impossible, so we left the children with my Mum and went away for a week on our own.

This was the first time we'd been away from the children for such a long time. Although we enjoyed the skiing, the holiday wasn't the same without them. But we had made a deliberate choice. This meant a conscious decision to separate from them for a little while.

When we arrived at the Italian ski resort there were more deliberate choices to be made. On the first day, the ski instructor gave us all a test to work out which groups we should go into.

We both started out on the nursery slopes, but I made faster progress than Barbara and by the end of the first day I had to make a choice.

The ski instructor told me to change groups, but this would mean spending every morning of our holiday apart. Neither of us wanted to do this. We had come away to spend some quality time together and this seemed to offer us the exact opposite. In the end, reluctantly, I chose to move to a more advanced group. Looking back on it, this was the right thing to do; but at the time it didn't feel very 'family-friendly'.

Having made one deliberate choice I found myself led into all sorts of others. There was the deliberate choice about risking the drag-lift: if I went on it would I fall off and go sliding down the mountain? There was the deliberate choice to follow the ski instructor to higher and higher slopes: would I be able to manage this next ski-run or end up in hospital with a broken neck? But the most difficult choice came on the Thursday. This was the moment of truth for me.

The ski instructor led us to the chair-lift that would take us to the top of the mountain – over 7,000 feet. One of the group dropped out. With legs feeling like jelly, I nearly did too. When I sat on the chair and was whisked off my feet, however, I made a deliberate choice to face my fear and take the risk.

When we arrived at the top of the mountain the view was breathtaking. We could see the Matterhorn and Switzerland in one direction, the Italian lakes in another. Then I looked at the glistening white piste. There was no way that I was going to survive this deliberate choice. As I slowly and gingerly inched my way down the fear of death gripped me like an icy fist. The only way back was down!

All through life there are times when separation is a deliberate choice. Some of these choices are made for us: the child leaving the womb; the five-year-old starting at school. Others are our own decision: the young adult setting up home on his own; the bride-to-be walking down the aisle on her father's arm. Many of these separations bring their fair share of pain, but Jesus can give us the courage to face them without fear.

As I made my way down what seemed like an impossible ski slope, in the eerie silence of the icy air I sensed God asking me this question: 'Robert, why are you afraid?' It was a good question. I thought about it as I turned, slid and fell; got back up again, turned, slid and fell again. Why was I afraid? I knew I wasn't afraid of dying; if I died at that moment I knew I would fall straight into the arms of my Heavenly Father. It wasn't death that I was afraid of, so what was it? I thought a bit harder.

Was it the pain of falling over or the fear of looking like an idiot on skis? No, it wasn't either of those things; I already had plenty of bruises and had long since realised that a beginner looks like what he is. Then it dawned on me: my fear was a fear of the unknown. I was afraid of the 'What if ... what if ... what if ...' effect of having made this deliberate choice. Fear of the unknown was robbing me of my courage, until I faced it with a deliberate choice to put the next few minutes into God's hands.

When our deliberate choices lead us into painful places, we need to remember the words of Jesus: 'I will be with you always' (Matt. 28:20) – yes, even when we are separated in our families by a deliberate choice.

2   Internal overload

We recently dug out our old pressure cooker from the cupboard so as to make room for other things. It was given to us as a wedding present and we used to use it a lot when we first got married. The mechanics of it are simple, but clever. A little water, a steady supply of heat and just the right amount of air pressure inside the sealed lid. The pressure is controlled by a device on top of the lid which acts as a pressure-relief valve. When the cooker has reached the right pressure inside, the valve releases the steam inside and pressure is regulated. Too little pressure and the gadget will not cook the food quickly; too much pressure and the results can be disastrous for anyone standing nearby in the kitchen.

Separation in family life can sometimes be caused by an

intolerable build up of pressure within us which can then lead to disastrous results.

This is what had happened in Jenny's family. Her marriage to Steve seemed ideal to those outside the home. They had two lovely children and a beautiful home on the edge of a sleepy West Country town. Steve had a good job with lots of prospects and the children were doing well at school.

At first Jenny didn't suspect anything. She was used to Steve's being late home from work; he often did overtime at the office to pay for those little extras like the children's new Hewlett-Packard PC. Then one day Jenny noticed something suspicious on the latest Visa statement. Steve usually dealt with all the finances, but on this occasion he had asked her to pay it off at the bank for him instead.

One of the entries detailed a transaction which had taken place at a nearby hotel. Her suspicions were roused. When Steve came home she asked him to explain the entry on the Visa statement. He tried to cover it up at first, but in the end the truth came out. He admitted he'd been having an affair with his secretary and the hotel entry was for a room they'd shared for a few passionate hours the previous month.

Jenny was devastated. She said nothing to the children but they realised something was wrong when Dad moved into the spare room.

In time Jenny learnt to forgive her husband and they decided to make a clean break and move. Steve was offered promotion and they had the chance to make a fresh start. For the time being the internal pressure on their marriage was released.

However, it was only a matter of months before Jenny's husband began another affair. She didn't find any evidence on a Visa statement this time, but somehow she just knew. It turned out that Steve had been a serial adulterer for the last five years of their married life – ever since their two children had been born. It all started when they hadn't been able to have sex during Jenny's pregnancy, but things had now got completely out of control. The intolerable build up of pressure within this family led to a breakdown and a divorce that hurt everyone.

Jenny still loves her ex-husband, and her children feel lost without him. But the internal pressure caused by his frequent return to this particular sin proved too much for her to bear. There are no easy answers to this sort of internal pressure and the separation it sometimes leads to. Jesus made it clear in his teaching that divorce is against God's plan for human beings. His teaching in Matthew 19:1–12 and Mark 10:1–12 looks back to God's original plan for people:

> Haven't you read the scripture that says that in the beginning the Creator made people male and female? And God said, 'For this reason a man will leave his father and mother and unite with his wife, but the two will become one'. So they are no longer two, but one. Man must not separate, then, what God has joined together (Matt. 19:4–6 TEV).

If we take his words seriously, then we must conclude that divorce is never a virtue. It may be the consequence of internal family breakdown, but it is not God's ideal plan for human beings. There is not space to do justice to this complex issue here. However, in terms of this particular discussion, we need to recognise the fact that some internal pressures become so great in family life that, unless something is done about them, separation will be the result.

By the time Jenny came to see me it was too late to do anything to prevent the separation in her home. It had already happened. Perhaps if Steve had asked for help when their sex life got into difficulty things would have been different. Maybe if they had both had marriage counselling after Jenny first discovered the adultery, pressure could have been released, forgiveness found and love restored. Unfortunately life is not always as tidy as this. Often we fail to ask for help until things have got out of control. Bringing Christ into the situation can still make all the difference.

Look at the way Jesus treated the Samaritan woman in John 4. It's a wonderful example of the way he works in someone's life. The story begins with a chance encounter. Tired and exhausted by the Mediterranean sun, Jesus decided to have a siesta. His disciples had gone into the village to get something to eat; he had stopped to sit down in the shade of a welcoming palm tree. It was about mid-day and all sensible people were keeping out of the sun's scorching rays.

The place where Jesus sat was a well-known tourist attraction. Jacob's Well was the famous place where Isaac's servants had got into a quarrel with the locals over water rights (see Gen. 20:19–22). Jacob eventually left the whole area to Joseph in his will. Centuries later it was still one of the best places to find water on a day like this.

Unfortunately Jesus had no bucket, so he waited. When a Samaritan woman came along to draw water Jesus broke Jewish custom and spoke to her. Men did not usually speak to women, especially Samaritans, who were considered by the Jews to be religious traitors. However, Jesus did not care much for religious traditions. He was more interested in rescuing people from the consequences of their sin.

This woman was no exception. At first they talked 'about the weather' and other 'red-herrings' which came into the conversation. It was only when Jesus brought her family into the conversation that their interview began to make sense. Jesus was interested in more than just getting a drink from this woman. He wanted to help her find the love that her present lover and the rest of her affairs had been unable to bring. She was living in sin, but this didn't stop Jesus reaching down into her life to set her free from the effects of that sin.

The conversation between Jesus and a casual passer-by may not look like much on paper. But it had an effect on the whole neighbourhood where that woman lived. When the penny dropped and she realised what she'd been missing, she dragged her lover, family, friends and anyone else she could get to come with her to Jesus. The whole city turned out to see Jesus and he changed the history in that place for good. Did the unnamed Samaritan woman leave her lover? We're not told. All we know is that many people in that area were never the same again. Her testimony speaks for itself.

Jenny's story is an all too familiar one today. Divorce was a route she felt she had to take to escape from the intolerable pressures building up in her home. More and more people are doing the same. Our job as Christ's followers is not to sit in judgment on them but to seek to show them by our example a better way.

Family breakdown is a great evil in society; it strikes at the heart of God's creation itself. But when we meet with it let us follow the example of Jesus. He met the Samaritan woman on her own terms, brought her face to face with the truth and then helped her find a way to escape from the bankruptcy of a broken home.

This is not an easy task, especially if the trouble happens to be in our own back yard. The benefits of bringing Christ into this sort of situation, however, extend not only to us and our family, but to our friends, neighbours and – dare we believe – even the whole city where we happen to live.

Then the woman left what she had been doing, went back to her family and told her whole community 'Come and meet the man who has helped me escape from the effects of all the bad things that I ever did. Can this man help you too?' She didn't need to wait for an answer; people came to Jesus in their droves (My paraphrase of John 4:28–30).

3 Death

William Shakespeare said through a character in one of his plays: 'Parting is such sweet sorrow.' I have often wondered about that much-quoted phrase. Can parting ever be sweet? Some people I have ministered to at times of bereavement describe death as a 'blessed relief'; 'they're at peace now' others say. It is as though somehow the most awful experience any human being ever has to face is suddenly something good.

The Bible doesn't say that. It's worth remembering how death first came into the world. When the members of the first human family turned away from God and decided to set their own agenda for life there were terrible consequences. This included painful mistrust in relationships, painful results in producing a family and painful trouble with the economy. But by far the worst pain was the experience of being cut off from eternal life.

Death was an intrusion into God's perfect world. God had never planned it to turn out like this. The presence of the tree of life in the middle of the garden showed that life was at the centre of it all. They had free access to this life. God didn't deny them anything, except the right to play God themselves. When Adam and Eve were expelled from Eden it was the beginning of the end. We are meant to read this story grasping the full force of horror in its terrible ending. Expulsion from Paradise was a tragedy of unimaginable proportions.

Eternity is written into the very nature of man, but because of sin it has been denied. As if to underline the seriousness of all this, the writer describes an armed guard at the entrance to Eden preventing any possible attempt to turn the clock back again (Gen. 3:22-4).

The whole of human history is written against the background of this vile interruption of what God had made to be so good. Evolutionary theory has got it right in one respect. Since the events of Genesis 3 humankind and the world we live in has been evolving – further and further away from God.

Human history is much more a description of decay than of progress. In a world of sophisticated human atrocities, it is simply untrue to say that people are better than they used to be. The human condition has not improved since God gave his ruling on the first family's choice of evil. If anything, as Jesus predicted, things are bound to get worse (see Matt. 24:3-14). St Paul summed up the biblical view of death: 'The last enemy to be destroyed is death' (1 Cor. 15:26). Death is no friend to any of us and we should never give it this sort of status. We were not created to die; God created us to live. When we die or any of our family dies we are experiencing the full horror of the effects of human sin. Is it any wonder that it hurts so much?

When my father died in 1988 it took everyone by surprise. It was October, school half-term had begun and we were due to travel the 260 miles from the Lake District to Bristol after Sunday services were over. On the Friday night I had phoned home just to check that it was still all right for us to come down to stay. To my surprise it was Dad who answered the telephone that night. This was most unusual. Whenever it rang he nearly always got Mum to answer it or someone else who was around. He was convinced it would never be 'for him'.

I can't remember what we said to each other, but it was the longest telephone conversation I had ever had with him. Eventually he passed me over to Mum and the details of our travel arrangements were quickly explained. As I replaced the telephone receiver, I wondered about my long chat with Dad. He was not a great conversationalist, even when you met him in the flesh. That made the telephone call all the more peculiar. I remember remarking on this to Barbara.

In one sense it was a very encouraging experience to have had. Dad and I had a very bad relationship when I was still living at home. But in the years after Barbara and I were married things had improved out of all recognition, especially when he had come to a personal faith in Christ in the last year of his life.

As we went to bed that night, I had no idea that less than twenty-four hours later Dad would be dead. Saturday was my day off and, as we often did, that day we took the children down to the lake.

Our home in those days was the vicarage at Matterdale. It is the most beautiful place we have ever lived. From our dining room window we could see Helvellyn in one direction, High Street in another, and just across the road from us the cosy protective outline of Gowbarrow Fell. It was a magical place to be, especially at that time of year. The autumn colours blended into the pastel browns and greens of the hillsides spreading themselves majestically in every direction. That day we had one of many lovely trips to the lake two miles away, collecting transfigured leaves, launching skimming stones across the serene surface of the lake, and pausing to drink in the wonder of what God had made. Death seemed very far away as we tumbled out of the car back at the vicarage and gathered around a sparkling

open fire for our tea. Then the telephone rang. It was my eldest
sister with some bad news. Dad was dead. He had had a massive
heart attack that afternoon and did not survive. The man I had
spoken to only a few hours earlier, was gone.

I am used to dealing with family deaths all the time. It's part
of my job. Howwever, it was quite a different matter trying to
deal with this one. I was stunned. Yet somehow the telephone
conversation, the plans to go to Bristol the next day ... all
seemed to fall into place. It was as though someone had been
ahead of us to prepare the way.

Death is the ultimate separation. It is no respector of persons.
It strikes when you least expect it and it leaves those around the
scene wondering what it all means. This must have been how
Martha and Mary felt in the story from John 11.

Lazarus, their brother, had died. Jesus was less than two days'
journey away when Lazarus had first become ill and could easily
have got there in time to save him. But he hadn't. He had kept
away and, some said, deliberately. When Jesus did finally turn
up, Mary couldn't bear to speak to him. She was confused and
angry. She knew Jesus could have saved Lazarus. She'd seem him
perform miracles before. He gave the blind sight, the deaf
hearing, the lame new legs and the hopeless, hope.

She'd once sat there, right at his feet and listened to him talk.
To hear him speak was healing in itself. There was something
about his words: so warm and tender; so filled with compassion
for the needy; so powerful without being proud or bossy. Yes, it
had been like sitting under a spell. Her sister Martha hadn't quite
seen things this way and had created a scene in the kitchen when
Jesus didn't send her sister to help with the clearing up. But what
a contrast his coming to see them was on this particular day.

It was Martha, not Mary, who was first at Jesus's feet this time.
When news came through he was on his way, she ran to him and
with a mixture of confusion and distress pleaded with him for his
help. Her words ran something like this:

Lord, if only you'd been here. We needed your help so much.
We called for you. We waited for you. We longed that you

might come before it was too late. Lord, if you'd been here, my brother wouldn't be dead now. You could have saved him, but you didn't. I don't understand why you've done this Lord: but I trust you. I've seen you do – well, things that none of us could ever have dreamed possible. Things look very bleak for us just now, but even now I believe in you. I believe that if you ask God he'll give you heaven and earth itself. Please ask him. Bring back Lazarus from that terrible place.

While Martha was pleading her cause, Mary didn't budge. She was almost paralysed by her grief: grief that her special brother had died; grief that they had been so cruelly separated; grief that Jesus had done nothing about it and had arrived too late. Martha knew what she was thinking. They'd aired their feelings many times over the last few days. It was bad enough losing a brother. She didn't want to lose a sister to bitterness, resentment and pain. Martha went back to fetch Mary out with words of encouragement like these:

Come out Mary; don't be afriad, Jesus is here. He wants to see you: don't shut him out; don't cut yourself off from him. He really loves you, you know.

Mary could be very stubborn. Once she'd made up her mind on something she was a very difficult person to shift. With some reluctance, she dried her eyes and followed Martha out. Her words to Jesus had a ring of grief about them:

Lord, if only . . . if only . . . Where were you when we needed you most? You could have saved Lazarus. You could have prevented this terrible tragedy from happening. Lord, how could you . . . You've let all of us down. If only . . .

Most of what Mary said was choked with tears. None of it escaped Jesus's attention. By now he was in no doubt about how this family felt, and he made no attempt to meet Mary's rebuke with a reply.

The sight of the grave triggered tears in his eyes. Deep emotions welled up inside him. He wept – not at Mary's misunderstanding of his motives; not at the stinging rebuke of those close by ('Could not he who opened the eyes of the blind man have kept this man from dying?', John 11:37); not at his failure to be there when his friends needed him.

Jesus wept at the awfulness of the death of someone he loved. As he stood there in the cemetery garden weeping, his mind went back to another garden he'd been in long before anyone around him had even been born. It was a perfect garden. A place to make you smile. A place to be at home in. A place that was just a pleasure to dig and to hoe. How many happy hours he'd spent there in the company of the people he had made . . . until one day he couldn't find them. They were hiding themselves in a bush and a covering of words which became their own grave. How awful it had all been: the sordid story of the slimy snake, the spiteful testimonies which made it look like everything was really all his fault.

It all seemed so familiar as he stood in this other garden and wept. This was what it had all led to: the expulsion from Eden, the judgment on sin, the fist raised in human rebellion returned to the dust from which it was made. Death was the reason Jesus had come.

The raising of Lazarus to life after being four days dead in the grave is one of the most gripping stories in the Bible. It tells us so much about Jesus and gives us dramatic insight into his attitude to death. In John's account of the story he uses the Greek word *splanchna* to describe how Jesus felt (John 11:33). The nearest we can get to its meaning in modern English is the phrase 'gut reaction'. Jesus had a deep-seated gut reaction to this interruption of his creation. It was wrong. It was all wrong. He had created human beings for eternity but rebellion and sin had spoiled it all.

Outside the tomb that day all the feelings of anger and horror at this unholy intervention of evil must have flooded through him. We need to remember this when death comes into our homes, as it surely will. Death was never God's plan for you and me and when it comes we are right to be angry, outraged and bereaved. But we also need to remember who is Lord of life and conqueror of the greatest enemy of humanity. 'The last enemy to be destroyed is death,' says St Paul (1 Cor. 15:26) and in Jesus this has now come true.

Bringing Christ into this dimension of family separation is the only, the most obvious and the overwhelmingly desperate answer for a moment when all hell seems to have been let loose in our home. Jesus has overcome the effects of human sin. And as we put our full confidence in him we shall find the lifeless tombstone can turn into a new door.

It was a crisp autumn day when we drove to the cemetery for the service that afternoon. The sun was setting over Bristol as we stood high on the hill where the gravestones fanned out across the ground. A westerly wind swept stray leaves around our feet as we made our way from the chapel to the grave. The full finality of death sank in as we passed stone upon stone with similar words of greeting: 'Rest in peace' ... 'Beloved husband and father' ... 'We shall miss you sorely' ... 'Fallen asleep in Christ'.

As I stood with my family around my father's grave-side we all sensed the pain and grief on Mum's face. But as the coffin was lowered and the words of committal began, I realised immediately that we were not alone. We huddled together for comfort from this most bitter experience, but the light of Christ shone out from the darkness beneath us. I could almost hear the angels singing those wonderful words celebrated in Handel's *Messiah*:

> O death, where is thy sting? O grave, where is thy victory? The sting of death is sin, and the strength of sin is the law. But thanks be to God which giveth us the victory through our Lord Jesus Christ (1 Cor. 15:55–7 AV).

Separation in family life is inevitable, but thanks be to God: with Christ by our side it does not need to be the end.

12

MY DREAM

Joseph was a dreamer. He had really big ideas. He dreamed of the future and what it could mean for him. The dreams he had didn't go down too well with his family. In fact, their reaction to them resulted in a twenty-year living nightmare for him. But in the end Joseph's dreams came true. What sort of dreams do we have for the future of our homes and families? In this last chapter I'll share some of mine.

My dream home

I have a recurring dream about a house I'm going to live in one day. It's a dream-house, set on the side of a steep hill. The dream begins with me walking up the winding driveway towards the front door. When I arrive at the door I'm not alone; my family is there. Together we go in to explore.

It's a wonderful place, but it's never quite finished. There are walls to be plastered, doors to be hung, windows to fit and rooms to be painted. As we go round it together there's a tremendous feeling of being at home. It's everything I could ever want in a house, including an upstairs lounge with a panoramic view.

Eventually the dream fades and I wake up finding myself longing for the day when the dream house will be finished and ready for me to move into.

What's your idea of a dream home? Imagine you have unlimited resources: what would it look like in real life? The amazing thing is that for each one of us the answer to that question will be different. We've been made by a God who has put the pattern of infinite creativity into our hearts and minds. He's made each one of us different, even down to the pattern of lines on our fingertips.

This shows itself in the way we live. Have you ever been into two homes which are identical? They may look the same on the outside, and even have the same room layout inside. But once you get past the front door everything is different: the choice of pictures, carpets, furniture, colour scheme, light shades, fixtures, fittings . . . they're all different.

We all express ourselves distinctively in the way we live. It's not surprising then that our dreams of the ideal family will vary. For some of us it will be 2.4 children, a dog, a cat, a budgie, and wall-to-wall Axminster carpet. For others it will be something quite different. But what makes a dream home is not the building, the contents or even the number of people in it. A dream home is where God's dreams for us can come true.

Dream people

To discover what these dreams are we need to learn to be dream people. This was the problem with Joseph's family (Gen. 37). They concentrated on the here and now instead of looking ahead to the future. God put dreams into Joseph's mind to prepare him for what was going to happen. His ability to recognise dreams and follow them led to a whole civilization being rescued. Think of it: your dream about your family could change the whole course of human history! It happened in Joseph's life; is there any reason it can't happen to us too?

We are living in an age of great uncertainty. The millennium is coming, and people are wondering what the future will hold. We get punch-drunk from statistics about marriage breakdown, child abuse, juvenile crime and population trends. As people search for some answers, we have a marvellous opportunity to share our vision of what Jesus can do when he comes into our lives. Let's face the statistics; we mustn't hide from the truth. But let's put the other side of the story too. Statistics are based on what has already happened: they are in the past. The future, however, is what might yet be. As George Bernard Shaw put it: 'You see things as they are, and ask: "Why?" I dream dreams of things that never were and ask: "Why not?"'[1]

Dream climate

To be dream people we need to breathe in a dream climate. This can be tricky. I once took a walk along the White Cliffs of Dover. It was a beautifully warm September day. As I made my way along the leas of St Margaret's Bay, I sat down on a bench strategically placed to make the most of the fabulous view.

I noticed that the seat had been given in memory of someone who really appreciated the sound, sight and smell of the sea. As I took in the scenery, I felt that person could have been me. The panorama was breathtaking. After many minutes of sitting spellbound by the dazzling beauty all around me, I continued my journey along the cliffs and down a pathway to the seashore.

When I got to the beach the spell was suddenly broken by the arrival of five mini-bus loads of highly-excited teenaged school children. This same 'dream scene' which once inspired Noel Coward and Ian Fleming to write and had captivated me from the cliffs above, was now inspiring them too. Their response to the scene, however, wasn't quiet contemplation but an explosion of activity as they swarmed across the bay!

The sudden invasion of those sixty teenagers made me think. Our homes are often places of conflicting dreams. Our children dream of us playing with them when we come home after a hard day's work; we dream of putting our feet up and unwinding with a nice cup of tea. We dream of holidays in a remote country cottage; they dream of discos and fun parks. How can we keep our dreams alive when other people interrupt them? Can we hold on to our dreams come what may? Let me take you to the other side of the world for some answers.

In a corner of the red-light district of Ban-Hwa city, Taiwan, 'The Spring' is open for business. It doesn't sell food, drugs, or sex like some of the other shops round about it. It's a place where street-children love to come for parties and stories about Jesus;

where street-people can get a shower to restore their dignity and eat some proper food; where the casualties of a sinful community find a home where there is no condemnation, no accusation and freedom from the past.[2] The environment outside is hostile; the prospects for many of the people, grim. But the values of this home give it a climate where God has begun to mend people's broken dreams. How can we cultivate this sort of climate in our homes too?

1 No condemnation

In my ministry I have met a lot of families with the wrong sorts of conviction. There's the husband who is convinced that he was never suited for his partner and sees his marriage as a great mistake. There's the parent who's convinced that the child born to them was an 'accident': unplanned, unwelcome and an intrusion into their world. There's the ear-ringed, undeodorised, spotty teenager who's convinced that his quiet, well-ordered middle-class home is the most 'sad' place on earth. And there are other homes where people are convinced that all their problems are somehow the result of God's personal vendetta against them. Their experience of life has taught them that the goodness of God is just a mirage.

Christ can free our minds from such negative convictions; his presence at the centre of our homes can create an atmosphere where personal nightmares like these are exchanged for some wonderful dreams. I heard a story once which summed up for me what this can mean in practice.

There was once a little boy who came into his father's study when he was working. Robbie knew he wasn't supposed to disturb his father when he was busy so for awhile he kept still. But his big brown eyes lit up as the sun sent a beautiful bright pool of light through the window. Pretending not to be there Robbie crept into the sunbeam, shuffling his feet across the shiny wooden floor. As the sun's rays beamed down upon him, his round chubby face broke into an ear-to-ear grin. Turning towards his father he looked up and said, 'Daddy! I'm standing in the smile of God.' His father looked up from his desk, locked eyes with his little one and took him into his arms.[3]

That little boy had the right conviction about God. His simple story speaks to us powerfully of the stuff of which dream-relationships are made. Yes, Christ came into the world to save us from our sin, thank God. Of course we all need to let him into the darkness of our human nature so that he can bring us into the light. But what then? St Paul said: 'If God is for us, who can be against us? Certainly not God, who did not even keep back his own Son, but offered him for us all!' (Rom. 8:31–2 TEV).

Once we welcome Christ into our homes we are bringing our wife, husband, children ... our whole being into the smile of God. That conviction will create a climate for some wonderful dreams.

2   *No accusation*

This speaks to us of an atmosphere where Christ sets us free from damaging sentences. Can you imagine a home where there are never any damaging criticisms? It's hard, isn't it? Phrases like, 'You've done that *again*', 'How could you be *so stupid*', and 'I *knew* you wouldn't remember what I told you' are far too often in our minds or on our lips.

We could blame someone else – like Adam and Eve – for starting it all. That's exactly what they did to try to escape accepting the blame. Adam pointed the finger at his wife, she pointed the finger at the snake and the same sort of thing has been going on in homes and families ever since. It's easy to 'pass the buck' and blame others for the situation we are in. However it's not the answer. Once we make an accusation it tends to stick.

That's why in Old Testament law a person could not be convicted on the basis of one person's testimony. There had to be at least two or three witnesses before the charge could be sustained (see Deut. 19:15; Num. 35:30; Deut. 17:6).

Believing in people is the way to create the right sort of atmosphere, where families can create dreams. Children have taught me so much about this divine quality. When they're little and they fall over and hurt themselves, they come running to sit on your knee. You hug them, rub the wounded area and say the magic words: 'There, there; all better now.' A few moments later, they are. Or perhaps their problem is to do with homework. It's a maths equation and you've never seen anything like it before. Somehow, together you work through it and the solution is found.

Children believe in grown-ups. They trust us, even when we let them down. It is this quality that can inspire the right sort of climate where God's dream for our home becomes a reality.

3   Forgiveness

The 'delete' command on a computer has formidable power. It can erase millions and millions of pieces of data in a split second. Weeks, months, even years of work can be erased at the press of a key. Christ's forgiveness in our homes is like that.

When Jesus came into the world to take away sin, his forgiveness went far beyond the surface. God's forgiveness pierces into the hard disc of our hearts where memories linger on. It wipes the record clean with the power of his love. The trouble with forgiveness that does not involve God is that it never goes beyond what's displayed on the screen of our minds. We forgive the sin, but remember the offence; the hurt, anger or resentment is 'saved' in our hearts. It reappears on the screen of our minds whenever the particular sin is repeated. 'I can forgive,' we say to ourselves, 'but don't expect me to forget.'

The effects of this can be far-reaching and long-lasting. I was reminded of this only the other day. It was Saturday night. I had taken a Sunday off so that we could spend a weekend at our house near Dover. The children were all settled down for the night, and Barbara and I were watching television. 'Are you going to make a drink?' I asked, expecting this unique person God had given me to share my life would suddenly jump up and fulfil my request. I was disappointed. 'In a minute. I just want to finish this,' Barbara replied, sorting the children's clothes.

Two minutes passed. Suddenly something inside me snapped.

I got up, stormed off to the kitchen and insisted on making the drink myself. I couldn't understand my reactions. I knew I was tired, but it was such a silly thing to make me over-react. Why shouldn't I wait for Barbara to finish what she was doing first, or better still offer to make the drink myself? We made up before we went to bed, but the next morning I woke up with the incident still on my mind. What was it that had caused me to react as I did?

Before anyone else was awake, I went to eight o'clock communion at the local church. Then I took a short walk along the beach. It was a beautiful day and the beach was deserted. As I walked across the shingle, my mind went back to the incident the night before. I turned it over in my mind and felt God searching the 'hard disc' of my heart.

Memories were retrieved from my childhood. I recalled how when I was at home, Dad hated making drinks for other people; he liked to be waited on. (So *that's* where I get it from!) On the only occasions that I remember his making drinks, somehow he always managed to leave me out. We had frequent rows about it, but it didn't change anything. In the end I began burying the feelings of resentment inside, 'saving' them on to the hard disc of my heart.

'Why did you react like that last night, Robert?' God asked me. Suddenly I knew the answer. Barbara's words had triggered off a memory inside. In an instant the resentment and hostile feelings had surfaced with a rush of anger. These feelings had led me into sin.

In some ways this was a very trivial matter. I felt ashamed of the fact that it had affected me for so long. But the incident taught me the importance of letting go of the past. Christ's love at work in us makes it possible for the 'hard disc' of our hearts to be wiped clean. The only way this can happen is to allow him to pierce the darkness of our memory banks, allow him to delete the data and then to restore us with his love. As the psalmist puts it:

The LORD is compassionate and gracious, slow to anger, abounding in love. He will not always accuse, nor will he harbour his anger for ever; he does not treat us as our sins deserve or repay us according to our iniquities. For as high as the heavens are above the earth, so great is his love for those who fear him; *as far as the east is from the west, so far has he removed our transgressions from us* (Ps. 103:8–12, emphasis added).

When we receive this forgiveness from God, and are released from the effects of the past, we are then able to convey Christ-like forgiveness to others. The best climate for producing dream-homes is one where Christ makes bad memories become a thing of the past. This brings us to the last of the four values we need to apply.

4   Freedom from the past

It was in response to a question about the future that Jesus told one of his most famous stories. A lawyer asked Jesus how he could make certain of his future inheritance. 'Teacher,' he asked, 'what must I do to inherit eternal life?' (Luke 10:25). It was a trick question; the lawyer wanted to catch Jesus out on a technicality and put himself in the right. Here was a man who needed to be exposed to the sort of climate we have been thinking about. So Jesus answered his need with the story of the Good Samaritan.

The setting of the story was a good choice: the road from Jerusalem down to Jericho. The people listening to him would have known it well. It was notorious for bandits. The road through the mountains twisted and turned, making it difficult to see possible trouble up ahead. When Jesus spoke about the unfortunate fate of the traveller in his story, none of his listeners would have been surprised. They probably shuddered at the thought that the person in the story could easily have been one of them.

As the story continued they could sympathise with the priest passing the casualty by. He must have been on his way back from religious duties in the temple and may well have had work to do in Jericho. Going near a dead body would, according to the law, disqualify him from doing anything for the rest of that day at least (Lev. 21:11; cf. Num. 6:6; 9:6; 19:11). They could understand the Levite acting just like the priest and not getting involved. It was a brave man or a fool that risked stopping on that treacherous highway. The idea of a Samaritan stopping his journey to help a Jew, however, must have made his listeners gasp. The only two things that Jews and Samaritans had in common was a border and their hatred of each other. What a twist in the story!

No wonder this was one of the stories Jesus told that people never forgot. The action of the Samaritan changed the victim's fate from no future to a new future.

The story of the Good Samaritan has a very powerful message for our homes and families today. Ever since human beings chose to abandon God's order for society and make up their own rules rather than following his, the world has been on a road going down from Jerusalem to Jericho. Jerusalem has always been a place of dreams in Israel. It symbolised the hope of the people of God (e.g. Ps. 122); the city which King David made into his capital (2 Sam. 5:6–10); and the place where God chose to dwell in his temple (1 Kgs. 6:11–13). It was the place where the Messiah would come to establish his rule on earth (e.g. Isa. 40:1–11).

In contrast, since the days of Joshua, Jericho has always been associated with a curse. After it was destroyed by the Israelites in the famous battle described in Joshua 6, it was meant to be left as a ruin for all time:

> Cursed before the LORD is the man who undertakes to rebuild this city, Jericho: At the cost of his firstborn son will he lay its foundations; at the cost of his youngest will he set up its gates (Josh. 6:26).

Four centuries later in the reign of Ahab, a man called Hiel of Bethel did rebuild it and his family life was ruined by death, just as Joshua predicted it would be (1 Kgs. 16:34).

As we look at family life in Britain today, we see it travelling

down from Jerusalem to Jericho: but it doesn't have to end up
there under a curse. With Christ at the centre of our homes, we
can make a difference. We can be there for casualties. We can
make our presence felt in society, showing by the way we live
that there is a better way. We can intervene with compassion to
arrest the decay and stop the moral slide down hill. And more
than all this: we can point people upwards to a new Jerusalem
where there will be no breakdowns, no separations, no crying or
human pain, and – no sin. Here's how one man saw it in an
amazing vision of the future:

> Then I saw a new heaven and a new earth, for the first heaven
> and the first earth had passed away, and there was no longer
> any sea. I saw the Holy City, the new Jerusalem, coming down
> out of heaven from God, prepared as a bride beautifully
> dressed for her husband. And I heard a loud voice from the
> throne saying, 'Now the dwelling of God is with men, and he
> will live with them. They will be his people, and God himself
> will be with them and be their God. He will wipe every tear
> from their eyes. There will be no more death or mourning or
> crying or pain, for the old order of things has passed away'
> (Rev. 21:1–14).

A home where people are set free from condemnation. A home
with an atmosphere unpolluted by poisonous accusations. A
home where forgiveness transforms all our relationships. A home
where people escape from the effects of the past. A home where
Christ is at the centre. This is my passion for the family. It is no
dream: it is the future.

Appendix A

SPECIFIC BIBLE TEACHINGS

In this appendix we look at some of the Scriptures which refer to specific subjects of a sexual nature. The list is not meant to be exhaustive, but it shows us just how much the Bible has to teach us on this subject.

1 Marriage

There are a number of references to marriage. Genesis 2:23–4 is one of the most important in the Bible. This text tells us that marriage was at the heart of God's design concept for man and woman. It was his invention, not man's. It is the most important relationship that can take place between two human beings. There were strict laws about who people could marry; most of these are in Leviticus 18, 20 and 21.

Proverbs praise the virtues of having a wife (Prov. 18:22, 30:10–31) and some of the potential problems too (Prov. 19:13, 25:24, 30:21–3). Jesus taught about the sanctity of marriage and based this on the Genesis 2 Scripture (Mark 10:2–12). Revelation uses the picture of a marriage feast to describe the final reunion between Christ and his people (Rev. 19:6–9).

2 Polygamy

Genesis 2:33–4 describes marriage as being between a man and a woman, to the exclusion of all others. This is the 'norm' or standard set by God; it is how he designed human society to function. Polygamy does occur in the Scriptures, but it is almost always portrayed as a departure from the ideal of monogamy. For instance, it caused trouble for Abraham when he married Hagar on Sarah's (his first wife) advice (Gen. 16). Eventually Hagar and her son Ishmael were forced out of the home by Sarah and became refugees whom, incidentally, God looked after in a wonderful way (Gen. 21:8–21).

Polygamy was outlawed in Deuteronomy 17:17. It was the cause of King Solomon's downfall (1 Kgs. 11:1–13) and ultimately led to the Kingdom of Israel being torn in two (1 Kgs. 12). Jesus's teaching assumed monogamy would be the 'norm' (Matt. 19:3–6) and on at least one occasion he sought to help a serial adulteress change her life-style (John 4:16–29). The early church taught the importance of monogamy as God's plan for marriage, especially with respect to church leaders who were expected to set an example to others (1 Tim. 3:1–2; Titus 1:6).

3   Virginity

The Bible sets great store on the need for chastity before marriage. A husband could insist on proof of virginity on the wedding night; lack of evidence of this in the wedding bed could result in the bride's being executed (Deut. 22:13–21). Priests were not allowed to marry anyone who wasn't a virgin (Lev. 21:14). Joseph nearly divorced Mary over doubts about her virginity (Matt. 1:19). St Paul taught that virginity for women and men was to be highly prized, and advised those who were under pressure to conform to the sexual customs of their society, to remain celibate (1 Cor. 7).

4   The sex organs

(*i*) Leviticus emphasises the need for scrupulous hygiene in relation to the sex organs. Careful sanitary instructions were given to take account of nocturnal emissions (wet dreams), other ejaculations of semen from the penis, menstruation, and bodily discharges of one sort or another from either sex (Lev. 15:16–33); 20:18; 22:1–8). We need to be careful how we apply this teaching in today's world, but the principles it contains would go a long way to making all sex between people safe sex. AIDS would be much less of a problem if society captured the spirit of this teaching.

(*ii*) A man with damaged testicles was not allowed to offer sacrifice in the temple (Lev. 21:20). Again, this needs to be interpreted with care today.

(*iii*) Abraham asked his servant to take hold of his genitals in a solemn oath (Gen. 24:2, 9). The same ritual took place just before Jacob died: he asked Joseph to take hold of his genitals as a solemnisation of the oath he was going to take (Gen. 47:29–31).

> 'Swearing by the genital organ . . . is a very ancient custom. It presupposes a special sanctity of this part of the body, which was no longer alive in the Israelite period.'

This idea of taking hold of someone's genitals to confirm a solemn oath sounds very strange to our twentieth-century way of thinking. I think perhaps solicitors aren't such a bad idea after all! But this ancient custom helps us to see that in biblical terms there is nothing inherently disgusting or dirty about the sex organs. Indeed God chose to use the penis for the sign of his covenant (circumcision): you can't get more sacred than that.

(*iv*) St Paul refers (indirectly) to the sex organs when using the image of the body of Christ to teach about the gifts of the spirit (1 Cor. 12:23).

5 *Nudity*

Adam and Eve were both naked in the garden of Eden. There was no shame in this until they had something to hide from God (Gen. 2:25; cf. 3:7–11). In the right context there is nothing to fear from being naked. However in some Scriptures nudity is associated with shame and disgrace. For example Noah's son

Ham was condemned for making his father's nudity an object of fascination (Gen. 9:21–2; see also 7 below). In Jeremiah, exposure to nudity is portrayed as something disgraceful and undesirable (Jer. 13:22, 26). Jesus uses the image of nakedness in Revelation to shame the church at Laodicea into doing something about its poor spiritual condition (Rev. 3:17).

6   *Coitus interruptus*

According to custom, a brother was under obligation to insemi-nate his sister-in-law if her husband died before she could produce an heir. This would ensure that his family would not die out and would provide security for his widow after he was gone. Judah asked his son Onan to perform this duty when his eldest son Er died leaving his widow Tamar childless. However Onan deliberately practised 'coitus interruptus' whenever he had sex with her to deliberately avoid getting his brother's wife pregnant (Gen. 38:8–10). This was a violation of custom and a serious breakdown in family solidarity. His behaviour so displeased God that he was put to death. His death was the result of disobedience, not because he practised this particular method of birth control!

7   *Homosexual sex*

There are various Scriptures which deal with this subject. The story of homosexual rape in Genesis 19:1–11 is by far the most graphic. The fact that it appears so early in the Scriptures reminds us that homosexuality is not a modern phenomenon. Gay activists are right to point out that this incident tells us more about the Bible's view of rape rather than homosexual genital acts. The behaviour of the men of Sodom not only offended against any civilised sense of decency; it was a violation of the most basic custom of showing hospitality to strangers. The graphic account shows that the Scripture is not timid about passing sentence on this sort of sexual behaviour.

Other Scriptures deal with more specific principles. Leviticus 18:22 and 20:13 show homosexual acts to be outside God's plan for man. They are condemned alongside all other sexual acts outside marriage. St Paul takes up the issue in Romans 1. He portrays this sort of sex as being against what God made man for and therefore a violation of his image. It is not natural for a man to copulate with another man or for two women to have sex together; this form of sexual activity departs from God's purpose in designing woman from and for man, and man and woman for each other.

8   Pre-marital sex

The New Testmanet uses the word 'fornication' to describe this (e.g. Matt. 5:32, 15:19; John 8:41; Acts 15:20; 1 Cor. 5:1, 6:13; 7:2; Col. 3:5). Both testaments make it clear that sex outside marriage is not God's plan for people. The law stated that a man who had sex with an unmarried woman was obliged to marry her (Exod. 22:16–17; Deut. 22:28). It is against God's plan for sex to be outside of a one-flesh relationship.

9   Surrogate parenthood

Hagar was a surrogate mother for Sarah (Gen. 16:1–4). This caused a lot of grief for all concerned when Sarah could not come to terms with the emotional consequences which followed.

10   Single parenting

God's care and concern for single parents is vividly shown by the way he took care of Hagar when eventually she was expelled from Abraham's home for good (Gen. 21:8–20). His tender care for Naomi and her daughter-in-law Ruth shows how much God cares for a family facing this sort of distress (Ruth 1–4). It is worth remembering that from such a home God raised up the greatest king Israel had ever had: David, from whose family Jesus's family was descended.

11   Sex techniques and positions

The Song of Solomon is hot stuff! It allegorises love and sexual
intercourse in a way that shows how good sex can be. It allows us
room to conclude that God wants us to use our imaginations a
little.

12   Sex therapy

I surprised myself on this one. When Isaac's mother Sarah died
he was, understandably distraught. Then God brought Rebekah
to him. They fell in love and when they got married the Scripture
tells us that Isaac was 'comforted' after his mother's death (Gen.
24:67). What a wonderfully caring God we have. Yes, good sex
can be wonderful therapy in bereavement and of course at other
times.

13   Oral sex

I'd be surprised if some couples wouldn't like scriptural guidance
on this subject. Read Songs of Songs 2:3 and 4:12–16 and draw
your own conclusions. The Bible makes sex something sacred:
that surely must include our genitals too.

14   Same-sex love

This is not the same as homosexual genital acts. There are several
examples of intimate love relationships between people of the
same sex in the Bible. We need not be ashamed of these. Rather
we should be saddened by the fact that today same-sex intimacy
is almost always assumed to manifest itself in genital activity.

   King David had a relationship with Jonathan that he described
as being closer than that of a woman (2 Sam. 1:26). Ruth was
inseparable from her mother-in-law Naomi (Ruth 1:16–18).
Jesus himself had a particularly intimate relationship with John,
one of his disciples. John describes himself throughout his gospel
as 'the one that Jesus loved' (John 13:23; 21:20); he rested on

Jesus's chest during the Last Supper (John 13:23, 25); he was the only disciple mentioned as being at the scene of Jesus's execution, and was close enough to Jesus to be entrusted with caring for his mother after he died (John 19:25–7). We should not be afraid of same-sex intimacy. There are moments in life when it offers us more intimacy than the best sex can.

15 Adultery

No surprises here. Sexual unfaithfulness is outlawed by the seventh commandment (Exod. 20:14; Deut. 5:18). The Bible could not be plainer on the subject. Jesus took the principle even farther by outlawing adultery by proxy, i.e. having sex with another person in your mind/imagination (Matt. 5:27–8). Beware when you see people having sex on television/video; you may be committing adultery.

16 Masturbation

This is sometimes called onanism, referring back to the story we've already looked at in Genesis 38. Clearly this particular story is about something else altogether. As far as I am aware, the Scripture is silent on the subject of masturbation. This is very surprising when you consider the strict teaching there has traditionally been in Christian circles about 'Thou shalt not do it'.

It is a perfectly normal and natural process of sexual experimentation and is not dirty or wrong. Provided it does not lead to over-indulgence or fantasising or take the place of healthy sexual relationships, we should leave people to make up their own minds about this one. As St Paul says: 'So whatever you believe about these things keep between yourself and God. Blessed is the man who does not condemn himself by what he approves' (Rom. 14:22).

17 Contraception

When God created human beings he gave them the power to procreate (Gen. 1:28). This was one purpose of sex. But Genesis

2:23–5 and Song of Songs gives us room to conclude that
husband and wife could enjoy sex without babies.

There are no Scriptures which support the idea that birth
control is against God's will. In some circumstances there are
clearly other considerations to be taken into account. Pharaoh
enforced a method of birth control on the Israelites in Exodus
1:15–22. This was an evil act on his part. But it does not mean
we should not use our minds to decide on the sensible spacing of
children in family life.

18   Rape

We have already referred to homosexual rape. The law prescribed the death penalty for a rapist (Deut. 22:25). Judges
19:22–8 and 2 Samuel 13 have vivid accounts of an incident of
rape and the consequences which followed. We can be in no
doubt about the seriousness of this sexual offence or of God's
determination to punish those who commit it.

19   Pornography

We have already seen that nudity in the right context is not dirty
or sinful. Looking at pictures or films of nude people and then
indulging sexual arousal, however, is covetousness: we want what
we see. It is sex without a relationship of love and intercourse
without commitment to the person(s) concerned. The law pro-
hibited coveting anything which belongs to your neighbour
(Exod. 20:17); this includes their sexual organs/experiences. St
Paul hits the nail on the head here when he says, 'Put to death
therefore what is earthly in you: immorality, impurity, passion,
evil desires, and *covetousness which is idolatry*. On account of these
the wrath of God is coming' (Col. 3:5–6 RSV, my emphasis).
Pornography will inevitably lead us into idolatry of one form or
another and endangers our relationship with God (cf. Ezek. 23
and Hos. 2).

20 Prostitution

This was forbidden in the law (Lev. 19:29; Deut. 23:17), but as with all sexual sins it is the sin which the law condemns rather than the sinner. Rahab was a prostitute, yet God used her to save his people from the King of Jericho (Josh. 2). She even gets a mention in the 'Who's Who' faith list in Hebrews 11:31. Jesus befriended prostitutes (Luke 7:39–50) and sought to help them overcome their sin (John 8:1–11). He had compassion for people who committed sexual sins, but was never soft on the need to turn away from these ungodly acts.

21 Bestiality

Sex with animals was a common practice for the nations the Israelites lived among. It will come as no surprise to read that the law prescribed the death penalty for people who indulged in this sort of activity (Exod. 22:19; Lev. 18:23, 20:15–16; Deut. 27:21). Enough said.

22 Voyeurism

King David became a victim of this when he was at the height of his rule and prowess. His adultery with Bathsheba began when he watched her bathing from the roof of his palace (2 Sam. 11:2). If only he had turned his eyes away, a terrible tragedy could have been avoided. The psalmist gives valuable advice to those of us like David, tempted just to take a look: 'I will set before my eyes no vile thing' (Ps. 101:3); 'Turn my eyes from looking at vanities' (Ps. 119:37 RSV). Jesus adds this piece of sound advice: 'If your right eye causes you to sin, gouge it out and throw it away. It is better for you to lose one part of your body than for your whole body to be thrown into hell' (Matt. 5:29).

What a lot of sound advice the Scriptures contain. Trust God's Word: it will be a light to your path and a guide to your feet (Ps. 119:105).

Appendix B

AIDS TO SEX EDUCATION

In this appendix I have listed some materials which are available to help families with sex education. There is a lot to choose from in the 'secular' realm. Some books are better than others. If I have included a book or pamphlet it is because I think it is at least worth having a look at it – even if it is only to help us to understand some of the thinking which is going on outside the Christian Church; we need to be in touch with this if we are serious about bringing Christ into this area of family life.

Having looked at quite a bit of the literature available, I am convinced that as Christians we have a unique privilege. We can with confidence present an alternative to the mainly amoral guidelines and information that you will find in most of the literature mentioned below. All the books were available in our local library or book shops. The material is not in any particular order of importance. Where I feel something is definitely worth buying I have indicated.

1   Lucienne Pickering, *Girls Talk; Boys Talk* (2 books) (Geoffrey Chapman, 1987).
This teaches children about sex through a story line that runs alongside some factual information. It was the only literature I came across which used this technique and on the whole I was impressed by the way it sought to portray sex as something which is part of everyday life. It was a bit forced in places, for example the way masturbation was introduced in *Boys Talk* (p. 47). There are some very good bits in it about the emotional side of human development, particularly with regard to girls' friendships. I

would not feel uneasy about recommending this to read with children, or even for them to read on their own (10+). However I don't think it is wise to let any child have a book about sex and give them the impression that they should 'read this book' to find out all about it. There is no substitute for talking about it in a secure environment. This book can help us to do this.

2   by Lynda Madaras with Dane Saavedra, *What's happening to my body?*, (Penguin, 1989).
This has a distinctive American style to it. It is honest, frank and (at times) too explicit. It was disappointing to find no moral standpoint, although the author makes no apology for her style. Her stated intention is to see things and discuss things from a son's point of view. I thought the best part of the book was the introductory section for parents. The 'Egg Assignment' was inspirational and well worth having a look at. Mind you, I can't see it working in some of the schools I can think of! I would not like to give this book to someone under 15 and would be very wary of giving it to any child unsupervised. I learnt a few things from this book myself but found one of the most helpful aspects of the book was its emphasis on openness and honesty in sexual matters.

3   Dr Miriam Stoppard, *Talking Sex – a book about growing up*. (Pan, 1982).
This has useful information in it at a young person's level, including a particularly good section about hormones and how they affect young people's feelings (pp. 34, 38). There are some revealing surveys in the book (although these are now a little out of date); the one on 'Petting' is worth looking at (pp. 56–8). Dr Stoppard gives some sound advice to parents about 'starting as you mean to go on' in respect of talking to children about sex. A particularly good section looks at the need for young people to take personal responsibility for their sexual activity and being prepared to face up to the consequences of having sex (p. 95 especially). With the exception of this item in the book, I was again disappointed that there was a lack of clear moral boundaries – for example the section on same-sex experimentation and stages

of maturation (pp. 65–7). Nevertheless, on balance, this book is well worth parents' consideration.

4   Eleanor Stephens, *Love Talk* (Virago, 1991).
This is not for anyone who is easily shocked! I wondered whether to leave it out of the list here but decided it was worth parents' attention in order for us to understand some of the attitudes towards sex that are around today and which are influencing our children. It is explicit and earthy in places; it doesn't pull any punches. The book puts sex at the centre (as opposed to love, faithfulness, etc.) and pleasure at the centre of sex. It portrays sexual pleasure as something which should be free from moral boundaries and sees no harm in fantasising or experimenting sexually during childhood. I would have problems giving a book with such explicit detail to someone who lacks the adult maturity to handle the emotions which accompany the sexual arousal it describes.

Although it has no ethics about when to or whether to have 'first sex', I was grateful for the line which said: 'Wait until you meet someone you love and trust and choose the time that's right for you both' (p. 36); as Christians we would want to add, 'Yes: and the right time is marriage.' There is a helpful section called 'Are you ready for love?' (pp. 36–8) and I rejoiced to find that celibacy was mentioned in a very positive light (p. 42); this was virtually unique in all the 'secular' material I studied. There is useful information about birth control (chap. 6) and some particularly good observations about learning to accept ourselves as we are – body shape and all (chap. 9). I found the chapter 'Coping with love' a very sad comment on marriage today: it is very heavily biased against monogamy. One passage has stayed with me: 'Keep a sense of humour. This is crucial. Some people say that God invented sex as a joke on humans! So never be afraid to laugh about it' (p. 42). I think it was worth my reading it just for the sake of this sound piece of advice, but I would not give this book to one of my children to read.

5   Peter Mayle, *What's happening to me? A guide to puberty* (Pan, 1993).

This book has certainly stood the test of time. It has some very clear, factual and sensitive material in it. Children will find it very accessible and practical. My main criticism of it is its very disappointing ending. Once again there are no clear moral guidelines and I found the closing remarks a lost opportunity: 'Part of falling in love is sex. When love and sex are combined, they make up what has to be one of the best feelings in the world. Enjoy it. Take good care of yourself. And good luck.'

6   Rosemary Stones, *Loving encounters – a book for teenagers about sex* (Picadilly, 1988).

I found very little to recommend this book but have included it because it contains a useful section on the law (though since it was published the age of consent for homosexual sex has come down now from 21 to 18). There is also a small but sensitive section about 'Sex and disability' (p. 75). It is almost devoid of any moral guidelines.

7   M. and M. Doney, *Who made me?* (Marshall Pickering).

This book should definitely be on your bookshelves. It is the best book I have come across for using with younger children. It has been well produced with good visual materials, is wisely balanced and, most importantly, is rooted in a scriptural context. It is worth reading other books just to appreciate the difference Christ makes when he is brought into sex education.

8   Ruth Thomson, *Have you started yet?* (Pan, 1987).

Good for parents, particularly fathers who want to understand more about the onset of puberty in girls. There is a very good chapter on how puberty affects the human body shape and layout. Lots of very practical information about sanitary hygiene and the experience of the first period. Well worth having on your bookshelves.

9   Tim Stafford, *Love sex and the whole person* (Campus Life, 1991).

I have found Tim Stafford's books enormously helpful, full of practical advice and biblically down to earth. This book is no exception: it is excellent for those of us with older teenagers. It is a good resource book for parents and teenagers alike and has the most balanced treatment of controversial subjects, such as masturbation and oral sex, that I have come across. A definite 'must have'!

10 Sue Meredith, *Growing Up* (Usborne, 1991).
Good visual presentation of sexual information in the classic Usborne style. I found the material easy to read and at a level most children could understand. There is a particularly good section on other related matters such as diet, exercise and personal hygiene (pp. 34ff.).

11 Roger & Christine Day, *Help! I'm growing up* (Harvestime, 1990).
This is a very practical, biblically-based book. The chapter on 'The price of sexual freedom' is one all parents and children should look at; it makes sobering reading. There is some very sensible advice about involuntary erections and ejaculations (pp. 62–4), suitable clothing (chap. 14) and lots of Bible study material. In places I found the guidance given a bit too cut and dried, and was disappointed that the authors treated masturbation as sin (see Tim Stafford above). The authors wisely make the point that parents may take a different view about this and other subjects, and this underlines the importance of reading books about sex with our children. There is a very helpful index to the book.

12 Michael Lawson and Dr David Skipp, *Sex and that* (Lion)
This book answers children's questions about sex in a straightforward manner. It is a short book which a child of 9+ should be able to cope with, although once again parents should read with their child. The information is set firmly in a Christian framework and I have no hesitation in recommending it for parents. It will need to be supplemented with other literature as well.

13 Kathy McCoy and Dr Charles Wibbelsman, *The Teenage Body Book* (Judy Piatkus, 1989).
This is an exhaustive textbook dealing with answers to questions teenagers ask about sex. In contrast to Tim Stafford's book it

does not adopt a clear moral approach, but it does have some encouraging comments in it about the value of virginity (pp. 54–5), 'Twelve good reasons to say "No" to sexual activity right now' (pp. 193–5), making love without having sex (pp. 198–9) and a discussion of some of the issues relating to homosexuality (pp. 188–90). There is also a good section on understanding adolescent feelings including a useful part on 'Stress' (pp. 76–80). Once again, as with so many modern secular books about sex, there is a profound lack of moral guidance in this book. However it is worth a look.

Also worth looking at;

These books are not specifically on sex but have some useful chapters in them. They are all (except for the book by Dr Spock) based on Christian teaching.

14   Janet and John Haughton, *Parenting Teenagers* (Kingsway, 1994).
Part Three on 'Love, Sex and Mirages' has some very helpful advice in it on practising what you preach, making use of everyday opportunities to raise the subject of sex, and sensible advice about handling pornography. Parents with teenagers will also value the other material in this book.

15   Dr Roger Hurding, *Understanding Adolescence* (Hodder & Stoughton, 1989).
This book is well researched and has suggestions for further reading on subjects raised. Chapters 6 and 7 are particularly relevant and cover a whole range of sexual matters from a theological basis. A book for parents who want to understand their teenagers, but not one that I would give to a child to read.

16   James Dobson, *The new Dare to Discipline* (Kingsway, 1993).
This book was first published in 1972 in Britain! It is a classic and has stood the test of time. It is inevitably American in style, but this should not put us off having it on our list of 'must have'

books. It has all sorts of helpful advice which I have found useful and effective throughout our family life. The penultimate chapter on morality is very direct and challenging. The statistics are American, but we can see similar trends in this country. I particularly liked the section on virginity (pp. 155–62). This book is for parents rather than children and is essential reading – but be aware there are some cultural differences.

17   Jeremie Hughes, *Will my rabbit go to heaven?* (Lion, 1992)
This book has been reprinted a number of times and it is not hard to see why. It begins with the sort of questions which children really ask. The last chapter is about sex and the family and is unmissable! Well worth buying.

18   Dr Benjamin Spock and Dr Michael Rothenberg, *Dr Spock's Baby and Child Care for the nineties* (Simon & Schuster, 1992).
I have included this here because it is a classic on child care. Although it is not written from a biblical standpoint, I found the section on sexual matters (pp. 485–514) refreshingly moral after reading some of the other 'secular' books mentioned above. Dr Spock has sometimes had a bad press in the past, but there is some very sound wisdom in this book and it is worth having.

Appendix C

PUBERTY QUIZ

Fill in the answers in the boxes provided

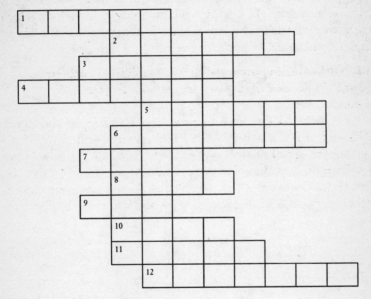

1 These start to be produced by the million in males.
2 The 'growth spurt' causes an increase in ....
3 This lengthens and thickens during a boy's puberty.
4 These grow and develop during a girl's puberty.
5 These start to produce sperm.
6 Hair appears in these in both boys and girls.
7 One of these starts to be released from an ovary during puberty.
8 Pubic .... appears during puberty.
9 An extra layer of this develops during puberty in girls.
10 These widen during a girl's puberty.
11 This will deepen and 'break' during a boy's puberty.
12 These grow and sometimes darken during breast development.

Answers to puberty quiz

1 Sperm
2 Height
3 Penis
4 Breasts
5 Testes
6 Armpits
7 Ovum
8 Hair
9 Fat
10 Hips
11 Voice
12 Nipples

Appendix D

PUBERTY WORD SEARCH

```
T  E  S  T  I  C  L  E  S  X  G  S
B  O  P  B  R  X  B  O  C  N  R  M
O  P  E  N  I  S  A  E  R  O  O  A
D  U  R  I  Y  R  A  V  O  I  W  E
Y  B  M  O  O  D  Y  O  T  S  T  D
O  I  S  W  E  A  T  U  U  I  H  D
D  C  X  T  U  V  R  W  M  C  S  T
O  H  Y  S  U  R  E  T  U  M  P  E
U  A  Z  E  F  H  B  G  I  U  R  W
R  I  N  P  S  T  U  Q  V  C  R  W
A  R  B  C  D  E  P  F  G  R  T  H
I  J  V  A  G  I  N  A  M  I  K  L
N  S  T  O  P  S  O  P  Q  C  R  S
M  E  N  S  T  R  U  A  T  I  O  N
```

Find the following words

Circumcision
Testicles
Sperm
Penis
Scrotum
Pubic Hair
Wet Dreams
Sweat
Growth Spurt

Body Odour
Moody
Puberty
Vagina
Uterus
Ovary
Spots
Menstruation

NOTES

Chapter 1: Help!

1 *Alternative Service Book* (The Central Board of Finance of the Church of England, 1980), p. 245.

Chapter 2: Home Truths

1 William Cowper, 'God Moves in A Mysterious Way' (1774).
2 I am indebted to Selwyn Hughes for this loose but brilliant paraphrase of what Adam actually said (Gen. 2:23).

Chapter 3: Good Sex

1 International Children's Bible (Wood Publishing, 1983, 1988).
2 K. Wellings, J. Field, A. M. Johnson and J. Wadsworth, *Sexual Behaviour in Britain* (Penguin, 1994), p. 84.
3 *ibid.*, p. 40.
4 *ibid.*, pp. 46, 48.
5 *ibid.*, p. 245.
7 G. Hauer, *Longing for Tenderness* (Editions Trobish, 1983).
8 *Sexual Behaviour*, *op. cit.*, p. 249.
9 *ibid.*, p. 71.
10 *ibid.*, p. 35.
11 M. Mason, *The Mystery of Marriage* (Marc Europe, 1985), pp. 121, 122.
12 Dr Miriam Stoppard, *Talking Sex: A book about growing up* (Pan, 1982), pp. 89–90.
13 *ibid.*, p. 92.

Chapter 4: God's Family Plan

1 G. von Rad, *Genesis* (SCM, 1961, 1972), pp. 88, 89.

Chapter 6: Chaos

1 This is a Cumbrian expression used to describe people having a chat over the garden fence or similar.

Chapter 10: Family Worship

1 O. Hallesby, *Prayer* (IVP, 1993), pp. 10–12.
2 Peter Brierley, *Reaching and Keeping Teenagers* (Marc, 1993).
3 John and Sue Ritter, *The Brat Pack*, (Marshall Pickering, 1994), pp. 86–7.

Chapter 11: Separation

1 High Street is the name given to one of the mountains in the Lake District above Lake Ullswater.

Chapter 12: My Dream

1 G. B. Shaw, cited in 'Church Leadership – a one-day seminar', *Visionary Leadership* (Marc Europe), p. 1.
2 I am grateful to Christine Hartley and Debbie Glick (formerly OMF missionaries serving in Taiwan) for these 'key values' which have inspired me and others to believe that God can mend broken dreams and broken lives.
3 I am indebted to Dr Marion Ashton for the quote on which this story is based. It comes from the first in a series of talks entitled 'Loved with an Everlasting Love', © CPAS, Athena Drive, Tachbrook Park, Warwick, CV34 6NG.